Martial Arts Master
KORI HISATAKA
My father's life in Manchuria

Sachiko Hisataka

Spiritual Development of Individuality in Mind and Body

Dedicated to my father and mother

Copyright © 2016 by Sachiko Hisataka

Martial Arts Master KORI HISATAKA:
My father's life in Manchuria

Translater: Hidemi Uebayashi
Editor: John Spiri

Published by Babel Press U.S.A.
All rights reserved

ISBN: 978-0989232685

Babel Corporation
Pacific Business News Bldg. #208,
1833 Kalakaua Avenue, Honolulu, Hawaii 96815

Preface

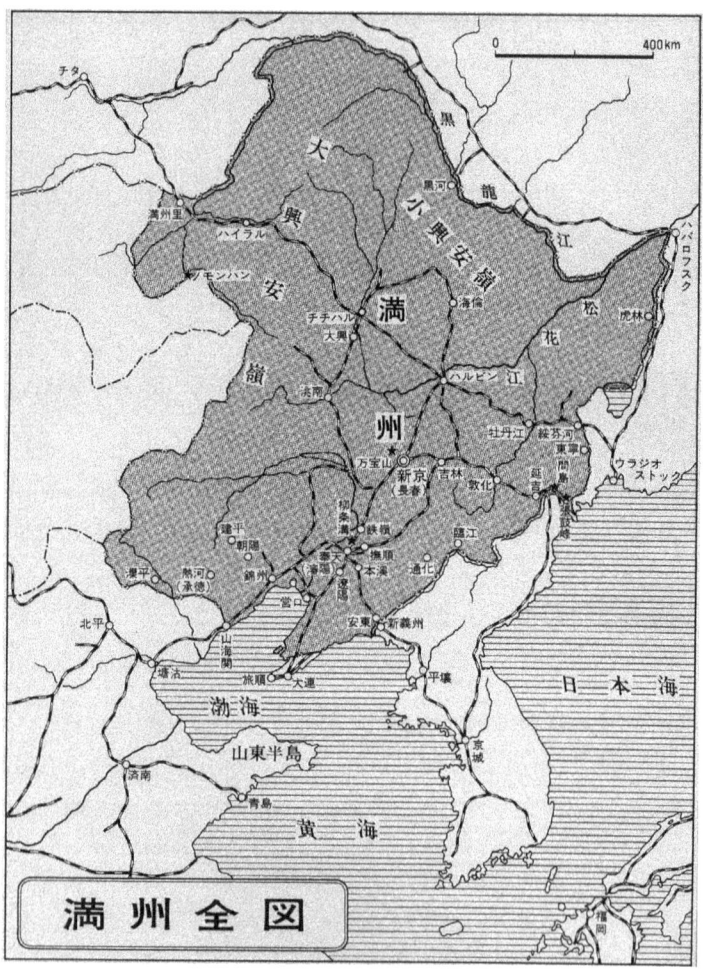

Map of Manchukuo

Dear Father,

I am standing on the Badaling section of the Great Wall.

People say, "The Great Wall of China is the only man-made construction on Earth that can be spotted from the moon," so I believe you can see it from heaven.

Do you see the strip that looks like a thin, pale-brown ribbon running along the surface of our blue Earth?

That is the Great Wall.

The countless clusters of black dots that look like tiny sesame seeds on the thin ribbon are tourists.

One of the black dots is me.

At last I have returned to the Great Wall that I had dreamed of all these years.

Now I am surrounded by crowds of tourists in colorful clothes. I see Chinese people. I see Japanese people. I also see Western people. The high-pitched voices of vendors are making the Wall as lively as a festival.

With the dark blue sky spreading over the green mountains in the far distance, the Great Wall runs from mountain to mountain, winding at many points as if it extends into infinity.

The furthest point of the Wall resembles a white band of light rising up into the heavens.

Oh, a small airplane has appeared out of white clouds and is flying straight toward me. Its silver wings are shining brightly under the sunlight. It seems to be a Japanese military plane.

Father, it's me, 70 years ago, on that plane, isn't it? It's me, still an infant, who was on a Japanese military plane on my mother's knees. I am the record holder as the youngest Japanese to fly over the Great Wall. This record will never be broken because a Japanese military plane will never fly over the Great Wall again.

Badaling has a long history as a battlefield since ancient times, especially as the location where the Japanese and Chinese armies fought fiercely until much blood was shed and many lives were lost. Now it has become one of the world's most popular sightseeing spots, teeming with tourists.

One of the mountains extends far past the Wall into Inner Mongolia, all the way to my birthplace in Zhangjiakou, doesn't it?

Father, I am poised to begin my journey to retrace your footsteps and fly over the Badaling Great Wall again to visit the land where I was born.

Scenes embedded in my memory

When my mother flew over the Great Wall to Zhangjiakou, where my father had been sent, I had not been born yet. She had one child born in Harbin, an 18-month old baby girl, on her back.

It was in early fall of 1938, 14 months after the Marco Polo Bridge Incident.

For seven years after that, until August 1945, my parents lived in a town far away from the Great Wall.

I believe everyone feels that the place where they were born, their birthplace, is their sacred place. My sacred place is located on the far side of the Great Wall.

I can recall the spacious, peaceful scenery, typical to Asia, from my distant past, memories embedded in my consciousness. In my memory I am often riding on a rickshaw. No, we called it a *yangche*, not a rickshaw. On a rumbling *yangche*, I traveled the path that appeared to continue into infinity.

There were some frigid mornings. Other times the car rumbled on the road between the vast green grasslands, rumbling toward the red evening sun. In those scenes, I, a small girl, am held on the knees of my mother or my father.

Such peaceful scenes were blown away in one instant in the storm of Japan's defeat in the War and our withdrawal from China.

After the storm has ended and many years have passed, as I stop and look back on the past, I find the Great Wall has always stood firm and calm, towering high into the sky. Beyond the Great Wall is the clear blue sky and grand vistas, even more perfect than the ones in my memory.

Those days I was so young so I can only remember fragments. Later, by talking about those days with my parents, and with the help of many records and documents, the scenes have gradually become clearer to me. Some of them can be recalled vividly, while others are quite uncertain, enshrouded by a dense fog. However, by connecting the certain and uncertain events, memories of my early childhood experiences have re-kindled in my mind.

Contents

Preface ... VI
Foundation of Manchukuo... 12
South Manchuria Railway Co., Ltd. ... 22
The Langfang Incident... 26
Harbin... 38
The Marco Polo Bridge Incident... 44
Zhangjiakou Railway Office... 50
The Great Badaling Flood... 60
The Battle of Wuyuan... 66
Fire at the Railway Company House on Dong'an Street... 74
Airplane Crash at Qinghe River... 78
Birth of the Son... 86
Yungang Grottoes... 94
Maidazhao and Hohhot... 102
Bao Taibao... 112
Soviet Union Entrance... 120
Total Repatriation... 126
The Imperial Portrait Train... 132
The Great Tianjin Riot ... 140
The Crematory in the Suburbs of Tianjin... 150
Tanggu... 162
U.S. Military Landing Craft (LST) ... 168
Arrival at Hario Seaport in Sasebo... 176

Epilogue... 184
Afterword... 196
About the Author... 198

Foundation of Manchukuo

Emperor Puyi and his wife arrived in Changchun on March 8th, 1932. Changchun Station was decorated with the flags of Manchuria and Japan celebrating the founding of the new state.

On March 1st, 1932, a new state of Manchukuo was established with Puyi of Aisin Gioro, the last emperor of the Qing Dynasty, as its chief official.

On March 8th, Puyi and his wife arrived at the Changchun Station under the tightest security. Welcomed by boisterous military music and people waving hand-held flags while shouting with joy, the couple marked the start of the new state.

On March 9th, the next day, the ceremonies of Puyi's inauguration and the country's establishment were conducted with all the pomp and circumstance one would expect. Even though people called the country a puppet state and the emperor a controlled doll, he demonstrated his magnificence in formal attire at the grand ceremony with the gracefulness of a former emperor of the Great Qing Dynasty.

The city of Changchun was renamed Hsinking and became the capital of Manchukuo. Hsinking residents were fully absorbed in a celebratory mood given the various festivities.

My father was formally invited to the state foundation festival, and participated in the kempo category of a martial arts competition held in West Park.

With Japanese and Manchurian flags flying, 25-year-old kempo practitioner Kori Hisataka performed in front of Chief Executive Puyi and high-ranking officials and governors from Japan, Manchuria, and Mongolia. He performed *kata*—choreographed movements—of Shaolin style kempo, *"kusanku"* and *"shishiryu no bojutsu,"* which brought thunderous applause.

Kusanku, also known as *happo-ate*, is a technique used when surrounded by opponents in all eight directions. It is a technique depending on quick and light body shifts executed without directly confronting the opponents' attacks. A practitioner takes full advantage of conditions such as day or night, brightness or darkness, the position of opponents, etc. Since childhood, my father was always highly skilled at this particular technique.

Everyone present held their breath and gazed intently at the sturdily-built man standing nearly 1.8 meters tall performing with grace and power.

My father's book notes that Kori Hisataka was initially named

Masayoshi, the third generation of Seison Kudaka (appointed as land steward of Kudaka Island and given the family name of Kudaka), a descendant of Fudai Daimyo Masaatsu Toguchi who was the lord of Nakijin Castle of Ryukyu that was first ruled by King Chinzei Hachiro Tametomo. His childhood name of *Masayoshi* changed later in life as was the custom at the time.

Kudaka Island appears in mythology as the place from where Okinawa emerged. In the age of dynasties, the successive kings regarded Kudaka Island as the sacred land of the creation of Ryukyu, and it was a custom to worship from a distance at *utaki*, a sacred place, on the opposite shore. It is still worshiped as a sacred island where ancestors are enshrined.

My father was born in April 1907. He enjoyed martial arts from infancy, and displayed extraordinary talent.

He was a distant pupil of Master Shinun Asato, and an immediate pupil of Chossun Kyan, the restorers of Ryukyu kempo. At the age of 12 or 13, he was already taller than 1.7 meters, and particularly strong at left-leg kicks.

He was examined for conscription, and passed as Class A. After 18 months in the military, he joined a martial arts demonstration trip across Japan and Taiwan in a group with his master Chossun Kyan. He then crossed the sea to Manchuria alone in 1932.

He was well known as "karate boy."

Departure to that region of the Asian continent, a vast desolate land, was his dream since infancy. His primary wish was to learn genuine martial techniques practiced in China, and at the same time, like many other young people of those days, he had an ambition to make a name for himself on the continent.

Father had been dreaming of becoming the ruler of Afghanistan. It must have been a great joy to him to have gained a chance to move to Manchuria as the first step toward it. Like many boys those days, he admired military officers. He had been studying intensively to join a youth military school until he fell ill with scarlet fever just before the entrance examination and had to give up on it.

While ill, he carefully thought about his future and concluded that, rather than becoming a member of an organization, he was more suitable for living freely in a wider world. He decided to follow his heart. This high fever might have been divine inspiration.

Having been brought up surrounded by the sea, looking far across it toward the horizon, dreaming of a wider, greater world, he chose to go on to a fisheries school. At this school he also polished his skill in judo. The instructor of the judo club immediately recognized his extraordinary talent in martial arts, and eagerly gave him lessons every day.

After practice at school, my father attended a dojo in town. He passionately devoted himself to practicing judo day and night. When the tatami mats in his dojo were worn, he brought tatami from home.

The members of his family were surprised to see the bare floor which their tatami mats had covered, but my father said that they could spread futons and sleep on them without tatami. In contrast, he explained, they could not practice judo at the dojo without tatami.

Before leaving Japan, my father desperately wanted to meet with judo master Sanbo Toku of Kodokan. To a serious disciple of judo like my father, Sanbo Toku was a god—or to opponents, a judo demon. This judo god welcomed a young man who had come from afar to see him without a letter of introduction. When my father arrived, Sanbo Toku was practicing at Kodokan.

Known as a lone warrior, Sanbo Toku was far larger and greater than my father had expected. "How about trying a match?" he said.

My father, overjoyed, tried to attack him. While attempting to grab his opponent, his body was in the air before he knew it. Wow! He was amazed to find that there was someone who was much stronger than himself.

While he might have felt surprise, it was only natural. His opponent was none other than the accomplished Sanbo Toku. However, even after being thrown, my father did *ukemi* and immediately bounced back up. Sanbo Toku grinned.

My father was thrown over and over, but each time he got back up right away. Even having attacked his opponent many times only to be dodged or thrown away, he did not stop attacking furiously.

After a while, Sanbo Toku beckoned his three strongest college students who had been practicing. All three of them held the 4th dan in judo and had massive builds. My father was told to have matches with them.

With three different techniques of *taiotoshi*, *osotogari*, and *uchimata* on respective students, he took them down. Sanbo Toku looked pleased. On that very day Sanbo Toku recommended that my father be given 4th dan in Kodokan Judo, and gave him the certificate.

The rank of 4th dan in Kodokan was an extraordinary title. Especially, the ranking system of Kodokan was very strict. Moving up in rank was very difficult. Even being recognized as 3rd dan was not easy. If you were recognized having 3rd dan rank, you could become a judo instructor at a junior high school.

The ranks of the 4th dan and above are the qualifications of *shihan*, master. My father was excited. In addition, Sanbo Toku wrote a letter of introduction to Shihan Enji Oki, a great martial artist residing in Lushun, and encouraged my father to learn diligently on the continent and be as active as possible.

My father's great fortune continued as Sanbo Toku was planning to visit Tokunoshima, his hometown. My father joined him on his journey down to Shimonoseki where the boat to the continent departed.

The large and warm figure of Sanbo Toku, who had bid him farewell in Shimonoseki, stayed deep within his heart for the rest of his life.

At last my father crossed the sea.

On landing in Dalian, the gateway to Manchuria, he visited Shihan Enji Oki. The great master of martial arts had already passed the age of 80 and had retired, but was still strong and healthy.

My father's move to Manchuria had appeared in the newspaper as, "Karate boy arrives on the Continent." That was how Shihan Oki learned that my father would visit him. He had been looking forward to seeing the karate boy, wondering what kind of young man he was. However, he did not show any hint of expectation when my father showed up.

White-haired Shihan Oki, in his chic kimono with *hakama*, appeared at the entrance and neatly sat straight on his legs before the front folding screen. With an iron fan in his right hand and his left fist on his lap, he said, "Now, attack me from anywhere," and calmly closed his eyes. My father was dumbfounded and stood still for a moment.

Shihan sitting in front of him showed no openings. He did not move an inch as if he had been sitting there for hundreds of years. The atmosphere was filled with tension.

A few seconds—or it might have been a dozen seconds—passed. However, those seconds seemed like forever to my father.

Shihan Oki had become like a stone statue. "What should I do...?" my father wondered.

After a while, my father decided, OK, I have no choice, and he threw his own bag with this fullest power toward the folding screen behind Shihan Oki.

The bag flew over Shihan's head and, with a thud, it hit the top of Mt. Fuji painted on the screen. When Shihan reacted to the sound very faintly, my father did not miss the instance and threw himself into Shihan's chest. Two of them fell together. The iron fan dropped from Shihan's right hand. He groaned and slowly stood up. Straightening his *hakama* with his hands, he called to his old wife in the back of the house.

"We have a guest staying over tonight."

After spending a few days with Shihan Oki, my father's karate performance tour in Manchuria started. First, accompanied by Shihan Oki, he performed karate techniques of *"kusanku"* and *"shishiryu no bojutsu"* at the Kwantung Army base.

It was very well received, and my father was given a reward worth several times as much as the standard starting salary of a college graduate. He tried to give it all to Shihan Oki, but his teacher would not accept it, saying, "They gave it to you, so you keep it." My father tried to persuade his master several times, but Shihan did not budge.

Then my father was officially invited to the martial arts festival to celebrate the establishment of Manchukuo.

His performance at the festival was much talked about, and he was welcomed at the succeeding performance venues including the police stations in Lushun, Dalian, Mukden, and Changchun, distinguished junior high schools in Lushun and Dalian, each local section of the South Manchuria Railway Co., Ltd. (known as "Mantetsu"), as well as the Japan-Russo school in Harbin.

One day, he heard about a master of a Chinese martial arts who was the head of mounted bandits with its base in the interior of Jilin Province.

Foundation of Manchukuo

He decided to go to see him on horseback accompanied by the head of the country border security police.

On their way, my father gave river water to his horse. Without much thought, he drank some himself and caught Manchurian Typhus. He was carried to Hsinking by a Kwantung Army military plane to Mantestsu Hospital. While in hospital, it was strongly recommended that he take the employment examination of Mantetsu.

My father had a dream of roaming throughout the continent leading a large number of followers, and becoming the head of Afghanistan in the future.

When asked why Afghanistan, he said, "You lack knowledge. Afghanistan is a kingdom and known as a country of *bushi*. I want to see what a country of *bushi* is like."

But he was told that Manchukuo would become an empire in the future, and its chief executive Puyi would become its emperor. It would be great to run around the continent with the bandits, but martial arts training and techniques should not just be for his individual interest but for the future of the new state. He was strongly encouraged to join the railway company.

It was much later when he found out that he had been invited to the company because of his excellent performance at the martial arts competition during the state foundation festival.

On January 15, 1933, my father joined the Hsinking office of the South Manchuria Railway, Co., Ltd. He was assigned to work for the Hsinking railway section.

His first mission was to be on board to guard the armored car that led the special train of Prince Chichibunomiya between Mukden and Hsinking on the main line of Mantetsu. He was told that they wanted to appoint him for the task, and that this was the reason why they invited him to work for the Hsinking section.

The garrison used to guard the railway roads, but after the founding of the state, Mantetsu was to guard its own railway tracks and trains.

After fulfilling his task smoothly, my father worked for the Hsinking section, and then the Tieling section. He was then transferred to Pingdingbao Station, the next one after Tieling Station.

It was a small station. When he was on the night shift, the sounds of horses clomping right outside the station were very noisy. The next morning he remarked to a Chinese man about what a terrible place it was, and was told that it was a path used by mounted bandits.

That explained why the interior of the station room was all fortified with iron plates. Sleeping there had been like sleeping inside a bullet.

He was told to experience working for both big and small stations to learn to be a stationmaster in the future, and was transferred to the Supingkai Station.

Manchukuo was founded spectacularly under the mottoes of "A realm of peace and prosperity" and "Five Races Under One Union (the Japanese, the Manchus, the Han, the Koreans, and the Mongols)."

Among those who founded Manchukuo, many had pure aims to establish an ideal state.

It was a new world of dreams that gave them great joy. However, under the rule of the Kwantung Army, an army group of the Imperial Japanese Army, reality would gradually lead them astray from the initial ideal.

"A realm of peace and prosperity" and "Five Races Under One Union" were ideas that really only applied to the Japanese after all.

The Chinese did not approve the founding of Manchukuo, and their rebellion to oust the Japanese intensified. Violent raids by anti-Manchurian and anti-Japanese guerrilla groups often took place. The raid on Fushun coal mine by such a guerrilla groups is one notable example.

If Manchuria was a "lifeline" to the Japanese, it was "life" itself to them.

On September 15th, 1933, three days before the one-year anniversary of the Manchurian Incident, the Japan–Manchukuo Protocol was signed by Nobuyoshi Muto, commander of the Kwantung Army, and Zheng Xiaoxu, prime minister of Manchukuo.

Here, "Manchukuo" was formerly approved as a state.

Guerrillas opposing Japan chose this signing day to attack Fushun coal mine.

In countering this raid, on the pretext of suppressing anti-Japanese guerrillas, the Japanese Army slaughtered the residents of the

Pingdingshan village, a village neighboring the Fushun coal mine. This is the Pingdingshan Village Massacre.

At around this time, looting cargo on freight trains was rampant at the South Manuchuria Railways.

Trains naturally lowered their speed at a spot where the railroad curved. Rebels took advantage and jumped onto the train, kicking the cargo out. Other members of the group waiting outside quickly snatched the loot and ran away. They showed surprising teamwork and could strike fast.

In addition, they were not just a group of thieves but organized anti-Manchurian activists virulently opposing the Japanese occupation. They were well-trained and elusive.

The garrison guarded the railways, but after the founding of the state, Mantetsu was guarding its own railways and trains. They tried various countermeasures, but did not find any solution.

My father's first working place at Mantetsu was the Hsinking section, the capital of Manchukuo. After his smooth service in on-board guarding for the special train for Prince Chichibunomiya, he was transferred to Tieling, then Pingdingbao, and finally Supingkai Station, devoted to transporting goods.

Supingkai had rich agricultural products in the west, and mineral resources in the east. The railway section was between Mukden and Hsinking on the main line of Mantetsu, and a key junction of the Pingqi line (between Supingkai and Qiqihar) and the Pingmei line (between Supingkai and Meihekou). Supingkai was a large distribution center for goods, and the station was important for freight transportation.

This means that there was no end to looting of freight trains around Supingkai Station. Thus, Supingkai Station decided to send young staff members, including my father, to catch the looters.

My father was the leader.

First, he asked the guards and police for cooperation.

Next, he gathered the finest spotters from among *tairiku ronin*, the Japanese who lived or roamed around China and the Korean Peninsula. They had bountiful energy and were impatiently waiting for incidents to happen. They longed for a wild adventure.

My father hid them among goods on an open car of a freight train. This was his strategy: when the train lowered its speed and just before the looters tried to jump on board, they would jump off the train to block the looters. While they grabbed and fought with each other, the guardsmen and police who had been hiding at a distance would come and arrest the looters.

This strategy worked well, and the looters were all arrested at the same time. The freight train passed by as if nothing happened. There was no trouble or delay to the train's operation.

Even though it was such a big incident, the train driver did not notice anything. Later, he regretted not knowing about the plan beforehand and said he would have cooperated. My father said that he had not told anything to the driver on purpose. If the driver had known, he very possibly would have done something unusual while operating the train.

Those looters were respected adversaries. They would have noticed anything unusual.

On my father's memory was imprinted the expression on the face of the ringleader of the looters when he was arrested.

He was held by both arms by the police, with his eyes wide-open in full rage. He glared at my father and said angrily, "We took one or two small parcels and you call us thieves, but who are the thieves? Just you wait. We will take this country, this land, back!"

South Manchuria Railway Co., Ltd.

"The Asia Express," the pride of Mantetsu

On March 23rd, 1935, the Soviet Union formally transferred complete ownership of the Manchurian Railway Lines (1,700 kilometers of the line connecting Hsinking, Harbin, and Heihe, and the line connecting Suifenhe and Manzhouli), as well as its additional facilities and property, to Manchukuo, which assigned the South Manchuria Railway Co., Ltd. (abbreviated as Mantetsu) to manage the operation.

My father had been working for Supingkai Station at that time. However, as Mantetsu took over the railway from the Soviet Union, he was transferred to Harbin as a commander of train operations.

Requisition proceeded smoothly and amicably.

Those who were leaving were of the mindset: "A bird taking flight does not foul the water," and those taking over understood such feeling and tried to meet expectations. Both sides devoted themselves to their tasks with pride as railway workers.

My father had expected to drink vodka together with the Soviet crew, but they were too busy for that. The Japanese and the Russians calmly worked together on the shift. They ate brown bread together, patting on each other's shoulders saying *"khorosho"* (good), or *"spasibo"* (thank you), encouraging each other while laboring side by side.

The Russian railway workers ceased working at 5pm sharp. They worked during the fixed time. The Japanese, on the other hand, did not want to stop a task in mid-completion and wanted to continue working until arriving at a good stopping point. But without the Russian workers, they could not continue the tasks required for acquisition of the railway.

Therefore, my father came up with the idea of practicing judo after 5 pm and invited others to join him.

For the requisition of the Manchurian Railway Lines, workers skilled both in letters and arms had been sent to Harbin from each section of Mantetsu. There were many tough fighters who had confidence in their own skills in the judo club.

Immediately, three workers who used to belong to a college judo club joined him. One of them was Japan's best user of *newaza* techniques when he was in college, and the other two had also made their mark in college judo. Together with a former judo instructor at the police department, a former sumo wrestler, and my father, the group numbered at six.

They soon renovated the railway club in Harbin into a judo dojo, and practiced together every day from five in the evening until 10 or 11pm. My father made it a rule to eat at the canteen of the railway club every day.

One day, when he went to the washing room underground, he heard strange rustling sounds. It was such a terrible noise, as if rats were having an athletic competition. He went back to the canteen and wanted to investigate, but the mustached Russian waiter was acting self-importantly. The Chinese waiter was still a young boy, but quick-witted, and his service seemed heartfelt. My father asked this Chinese boy about the noise, but he did not know and brought an elder Chinese to my father.

When the Russian Empire built the Chinese Eastern Railway, of course the Russians were responsible for the design the construction, but the construction workers were Chinese. After the work was completed, the Russians invited the Chinese workers, saying that they would pay their wages, and held a party to celebrate the completion. However, the food served at the party was poisoned.

Although the exact number was uncertain, the victims equaled one or even two hundred. Party-goers died one after another, and the dead bodies were disposed of in that underground room.

That hellish underground became a perfectly suitable home for rats.

No one knows if this story is true or not, but whatever the reason, rats have enjoyed a free life there running around since that time.

My father and his fellow workers shared their joys and hardships with the Russians. However, after the requisition process finished, they had to tackle the task of sending the Russians and their families back to their country.

When a girl on the Soviet-bound train almost dropped a doll, her arm was caught between the train doors and could not move. Her mother standing by her screamed and cried out for help.

My father used his full power in pulling her arm out of the doors.

The doll-like girl with her transparent white skin and lightly waved hair was terrified. Her large black eyes were wide open. My father would vividly remember her pale face ten years later.

Only God would know that Manchukuo, despite its promising future, would decline in just ten years, and he would fall into the position of slinking away like this girl, and would have to handle the task of sending the withdrawing Japanese back to their home country.

Ironically, what initiated Manchukuo's fall was the invasion by the army of the Soviet Union, the doll-like girl's native country.

On August 31st, 1935, after the requisition, my father took part in the great work that would be recorded in the history of Mantetsu. The railway required from the Manchuria Railway was a broad gauge (the track gauge of 5 feet). They had to standardize it to the track gauge of 4.8 feet (146 centimeters).

After five month's careful preparation work from the requisition, on August 31st of the same year, they successfully carried out the mission of narrowing the gauge of a 242 kilometer railway section between Harbin and Hsinking on the Jingbang line in only three hours, while maintaining the normal operation of all the trains.

At the same time, other facilities were also replaced.

The high-level technical skill of Mantetsu was fully demonstrated, a record in the history of transportation.

"Asia Express," the pride of Mantetsu, had been operated only between Dalian and Hsinking. However, from that moment on that day, it ran rapidly between Dalian and Harbin.

Asia Express started operation in 1934 at the speed of 120 kilometers per hour, the fastest in Asia. It was a dream super express with all air-conditioned cars, a rarity in those days.

After the requisition of the Manchuria Railway, now due to the Langfang Incident, he was told to go to Shanhai Pass in the stationmaster's office in Harbin.

Whenever an incident occurred at Mantetsu and railway workers were called, my father was chosen and sent with the phrase, "Because you are a samurai."

The Langfang Incident

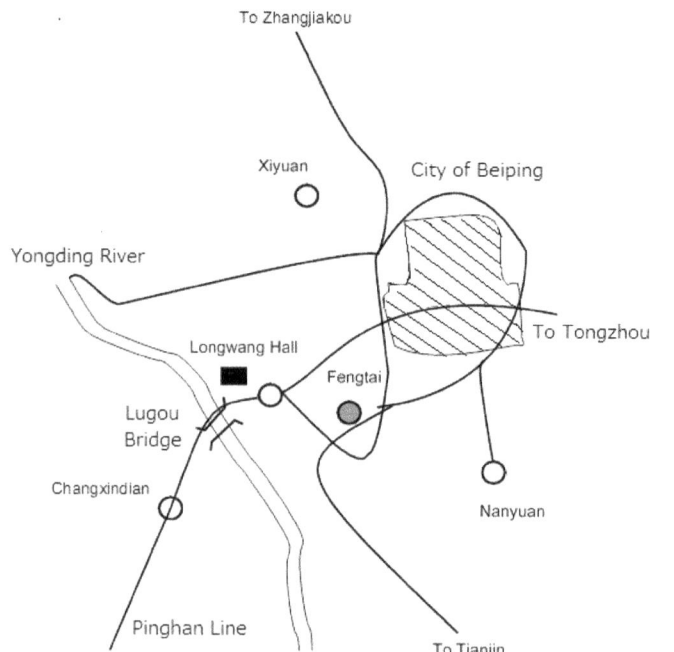

Map Around Fengtai

One night, about ten days after the New Year, an extra train with a large amount of opium ran nonstop from Hankou to Beiping. Various rumors and assumptions swirled about the operation of the train. Three theories dominated the speculation.

"Isn't it General Song Zheyuan of the 29th Route Army, trying to raise war funds?"

"No, surely it's the Eighth Route Army in the Huabei region attempting to raise funds to advance to Beiping."

"Wrong. The Japanese military police might have run it to procure the funds for pacifying Chinese rebels."

These speculations could be backed up by rational reasons—but none had evidence.

Therefore, the Japanese Kwantung Army started an investigation in secret to find out the truth. This annoyed the 29th Route Army. The investigation might give the Kwantung Army some reasons to make a false accusation against them.

Also, their confidential discoveries might be revealed to the Japanese military or others.

Therefore, to block the investigation, the Chinese military cut the electrical wires of the railway lines at Langfang Station. Mantetsu was in a panic. Langfang Station was located midway between Beiping and Tianjin, and the Pingshan line (Beiping – Fengtai – Langfang – Tianjin – Shanhaiguan) and the Mantetsu line shared operations at Shanhaiguan Station.

Shanhaiguan was an important point located on the border between Manchuria and Huabei. They had to restore normal railway operation immediately. Mantetsu called in 600 workers from each section and those doing fieldwork to work on recovery.

My father had been told in the stationmaster's room of Harbin to go to Shanhaiguan as a commander of train operations.

Soon after the repairs in Shanhaiguan Station were completed, on February 3rd of the same year, he was suddenly called to the stationmaster's room in Shanhaiguan Station at 9 am. While he was heading to the room, a stranger in a suit came up to him. He was wearing a felt hat over his eyes and black glasses. My father did not know if he was a Mantetsu worker or a military policeman.

He confirmed my father's name, and then commanded in a low, controlled voice: "At noon tomorrow, come to the platform of the Pingshan line in laborer's clothes with everything prepared. Be punctual, and keep it confidential."

He produced a brown envelop from inside his jacket, and pressed it into my father's pocket. Inside was a piece of paper listing the items to purchase and some money for them.

The next day, with purchased goods including a Chinese laborer's costume, a cooking pot, and a cooking stove, he was standing on the platform of the Pingshan line as he had been told. This time, a military policeman in uniform appeared. The policeman led him to a special room in the second-class car.

Sitting at the center with a shoulder badge denoting his rank as the staff officer, the major of Tianjin Garrison headquarters looked at a map spread out on the table. He was the man who would later insist on instigating more fighting at the start of the Marco Polo Bridge Incident, saying it was "a golden opportunity."

Military policemen stood on both sides of my father.

There were two other men who had been told to come in laborer's garb.

One of them was Kesasuke Oyama, a top-level Japanese-Chinese interpreter and the stationmaster of Jiamusi Station on the Mantetsu main line. He was 50 years old. The other man was Tasaku Iwaki, the assistant stationmaster of Hsinking Station, 39 years old.

These two and my 27-year-old father, a commander of train operations at Harbin Station, were the three men who had been selected from among 600 men to carry out the special mission. Pointing to places on the map, the intelligence staff major started to explain to the three about the situation around Beiping and their mission.

Stationed in Fengtai at that time were General Song Zheyuan and his 29th Route Army. Meanwhile, General Shang Zhen and his army were in Shanxi Province. Also, to the west of Beiping, in Suiyuan Province over the Badaling Great Wall, Fu Zuoyi resided.

If there was any hint that these three leaders were in cahoots against the Japanese army, their communication means with each other had to be cut off. Thus, the aim of this operation was to cut off the communication among the three leaders.

To fulfill the mission, first they had to investigate the movements of the 29th Route Army stationed in Fengtai.

Second, they had to accurately grasp the arrivals and departures of trains and the flow of human traffic at Fengtai Station. All information of even the smallest movement should be reported.

These were the special missions assigned to my father and his colleagues.

The three were ordered to infiltrate Fengtai disguised as Chinese peasants and spy on the 29th Route Army. They were to take care of themselves, cooking their own meals and the like.

Fengtai was southwest of Beiping, and its station was the first one from Beiping on the Pingshan line connecting Beiping and Shanhaiguan. It was close to the Marco Polo Bridge. Due to effuse praise in the writings of Marco Polo, this bridge, which is locally known as the Lugou Bridge (Lugou being the old name for the Yongding River), has become internationally known as the Marco Polo Bridge. The 29th Route Army and the Japanese Army were also stationed there.

Fengtai also had a huge station stocked with vital food, goods, and ammunition. As for their roles, Kesasuke Oyama, the Jiamusi Station stationmaster who was fluent in Chinese, was to negotiate with the Chinese Army. The other two were not allowed to speak with anyone, including both Chinese and Japanese. Accordingly, they were forbidden to speak a word of Japanese outside.

They were also told to greet the military policemen with their eyes only.

My father was to watch around Fengtai Station and keep records of departures, arrivals, destinations, and the numbers of all train cars. If the train was a freight train, he had to record as many cargo items as possible. He was told he could blow up the train turntable, the device for turning the train's rolling stock, with hand grenades.

The third member, Tasaku Iwaki, the Beiping Station assistant stationmaster, served as the contact with the Japanese military police. He was assigned to keep records of daily activities of the three members and detailed information gained each day, and then give it to the military policemen arriving and leaving the station platform.

The three of them left Shanhaiguan and arrived at Fengtai Station at half past six in the evening. They were overwhelmed by the vast station yard and the many switching rails. Across the rails they spotted a kempei, Japan's military policeman. He seemed to be watching them.

There were some low houses with mud walls in front of the station.

After greeting the kempei with furtive glances, they went into one of the structures, a cheap hotel. Local Chinese soon discovered that the three of them were Japanese.

Even though they were in ordinary Chinese clothes, their disguise was inadequate. Especially my father stood out due to the fact his clothes were too short for his tall frame. Word of strange Japanese men posing as Chinese in town spread rapidly.

My father went out to buy some food for supper, but he was turned away at every store. Locals had already gotten General Song Zheyuan's order to not cooperate with them. Therefore, from the next day, the kempei handed my father and his colleagues rice balls and salt.

The infiltration of Japanese spies set General Song Zheyuan on extreme high alert, and his army started to obsessively watch the movements of my father and his colleagues. Not only in the daytime but also at night someone came to watch them every hour.

The Chinese repeatedly asked questions that beat around the bush to get information. Each time Stationmaster Oyama replied politely, but he was often perplexed attempting to answer.

The questioners were in military uniform carrying bayonets. No one could tell how they would react to an answer. Also, if the Japanese showed a hint of suspicious behavior, they might take it as provocation. Still, it was clear that the Chinese were trying to provoke a certain reaction.

Stationmaster Oyama could not sleep. Various aspects of the mission stressed him so much that he gradually lost heart. Finally, on the fifth day, he began to unravel. On the sixth day, he was taken by the Chinese military.

He was released the same day, but showed signs of extreme fatigue, both physically and mentally. Unable to come to grips with all he had seen and did, he stared blankly into space.

Assistant Stationmaster Iwaki neglected his duty, fearing the patrol of the Chinese army conducted every night, and my father acted for him.

At dusk of the eighth day, when my father was taking a memo of the number of cars and their assigned numbers, he sensed someone approaching from behind. At once he pushed the paper into his mouth and crawled flat under a car. Avoiding gunshots aimed at him, he escaped by getting up and running between cars, finally jumping onto a train that had just started to pull out of the station.

Its destination was Beiping.

He knocked strongly on the door to the Mantestu North China office next to Beijing Hotel.

"Who is it?"

"I'm not a bad guy."

"A bad guy would say that."

"I work for Mantetsu and can prove it. Anyway, please let me in."

He forced himself inside.

The appearance of a large man in Chinese clothing surprised the man.

"Look at what you wear!"

"Do me a favor. Lend me some money."

"What's that? You must be a burglar."

"No, I'm not. I can't tell you the details, but I can't walk outside in these clothes."

"But you have come in those clothes."

"Please. Lend me some money to buy clothes and food for one week."

The man in the office told my father to wait a second and went into the back room to call someone on the phone.

He seemed to be confirming the identity of the visitor.

After a long talk, he came back shaking his head.

Still looking distrustful, he handed my father more money than expected.

After walking and hanging around restaurants and brothels in Wangfujing, my father thought it was time he could go back. He decided to return to Fengtai from Beiping Station.

When he got off the train on the platform at Fengtai Station, that

The Langfang Incident

contact man with the soft hat and black glasses grabbed him by the arm with a fierce look on his face.

He lowered his already deepened voice.

"I've been looking for you everywhere. Where have you been without telling me?!"

"I was almost killed."

"We are leaving this place."

"But what about the others?"

"The other two have already left. Hurry up and get out of here."

"OK—am I going back to Shanhaiguan or Harbin?"

Before he finished his question, he was decisively told to shut up by the man.

"Go to Tianjin."

"Tianjin?"

"Yes, Tianjin. To Furong Hotel."

"What will I do there?"

"Don't ask, just go. Wait there for word."

"What word?"

"A military command."

"But I work for Mantetsu."

"Don't be silly! The military controls your status."

"Why is that?"

"Don't ask. Wait at Furong Hotel for some time and you'll find out. And, remember, don't say a word about what happened here in Fengtai. Absolutely secret. Understood?"

"Yes." My father was harshly warned.

Stationmaster Oyama also suffered a mental breakdown and was sent back to his hometown. Meanwhile, assistant stationmaster Iwaki returned to work.

There were various guests staying at Furong Hotel in Tianjin. It also appeared that people in military uniform were frequently entering and leaving. However, the atmosphere was somewhat unusual, as if discouraging them to exchange names or disclose their identification. Guests were spending their days freely. He noticed the man next door was constantly writing something intensively.

My father later learned that Furong Hotel was frequently used by the Japanese army.

There was nothing more boring than staying in the hotel all day, all the more for someone active like my father. He went to a dance hall in the French Concession every day. As he was supposed to be waiting for a command, he visited the accounting office every time he went out. Each time they generously lent my father as much as he asked. At the entrance of the hotel, there was always a man with an unusually square-jawed face. He was a sullen fellow. He sharply glanced at my father when he left in high spirits in a crisp tailored jacket.

On the floor, one step lower into the darkness, on the shady hall, glamorous dancers with heavy make-up were standing in a row with their backs to the wall. Every time my father chose one of the dancers he liked and stood in front of her, she seductively stretched her arms toward him.

After one week of going to dance, he learned the steps fairly well.

Right after returning to his hotel, barefoot, he studied the dance steps he had just learned, comparing them with the basic *"neko-ashi"* (cat feet) walk of karate. This involved walking around the room to study footsteps (forward, backward, turns, zigzag forward, S-shape backward, etc.), body movements, weight shifting, all with special emphasis on gauging the distance to the most dangerous opponent.

Neko-ashi is the basic footsteps of karate, similar to the sliding walk of a Noh performer.

One day, the man next door who had been writing furiously talked to my father. Interaction with others was quite unusual.

"The dance hall may be fun, but can you come to my lecture tomorrow evening?"

He wore glasses, looking sensitive but intelligent.

"How do you know I go dancing?"

"Everyone staying here knows you do. Your manner is rough and voice is loud."

"Did I disturb your studies?"

"No. I am always impressed by your passion. I hear you are very skilled in martial arts."

"I appreciate your praise. OK, I trust you. I am happy to attend your lecture."

"I hope I can see how good you are in martial arts some other time."

"Yeah, sure. I promise."

"Can't wait," he said, smiling kindly. He approached the other guests at Furong Hotel and invited them one by one to his lecture.

The lecture was given at a Japanese school in the neighborhood. There was a large signboard at the entrance of the lecture hall:

Theme: "If Japan and the U.S. Fight"
By Shinnosuke Yamamura, Manchuria Daily News

"So, he is a journalist," my father thought. That was a little surprising because he had assumed the man might be a scholar.

There was a large number of people already gathered in the hall.

"I didn't know that there are so many Japanese people around here," my father thought, impressed by the sight. As he looked around, he recognized guests from Furong Hotel.

As they shared the same hotel, they knew each other's faces. The atmosphere inside the hotel was uneasy, discouraging them to talk to each other, but when they met outside, they felt close, as if meeting ex-classmates or someone from their hometown. They exchanged friendly greetings saying, "So, you were also invited?" They sat close to each other.

In the front row seats to the right of the stage, my father found the man with a square face.

He thought, "He looks unfriendly, but seeing that he has come to the lecture for the journalist, he may not be an altogether bad guy." He started to change his view toward the man.

"I regret not liking him for no particular reason." Such an innocent thought would soon be shattered.

The lecture did not last five minutes.

The journalist started his speech:

"If Japan and the U.S. start a war, considering the current situation between the two countries, specifically, fighting ability and economic prowess, there is no doubt that Japan will lose."

Japan will lose...

Yes, he actually said that.

However, that moment was not clearly remembered. What was imprinted on my father's memory was the moment after the utterance.

From under the right and left sides, four or five men suddenly rushed the stage.

One of them, the first on the stage, was the man with a square face. They jumped onto the journalist from both sides, pressed him down, and dragged him away.

It all happened in the blink of an eye, an almost admirable arrest, as if they had repeatedly practiced.

The audience was dumbfounded, not immediately comprehending what had just transpired. By the time the attackers finished, and the audience stood up making a stir, everything had already ended.

Without a word, Furong Hotel residents left the hall to lethargically return to the hotel, everyone staying close together as if they were a group of lambs being led to a slaughterhouse.

No one felt like going back to their own room. Although no one suggested it, they ended up gathering in the dining room.

Without speaking, they were lost in their own thoughts.

"Why and until when am I made to stay here at Furong Hotel?" my father wondered.

Everyone had his own reasons for staying there.

My father was looking back at the meeting with the intelligence staff major he met at Shanhaiguan Station and what had happened at Fengtai Station.

When he went to the washroom the next morning, the square-faced man was brushing his teeth slowly, as if nothing had happened.

Rumors swirled about town that the journalist had been shot and killed before dawn.

In early afternoon, the contact man with black glasses came hastily. He was usually commanding and calm, but on this particular day he was upset. He asked my father if he had been friends with the journalist next door, and if he had only been invited to the previous night's lecture. The man repeated the same questions several times and finally asked my father if he had received anything from the journalist.

My father was offended by his persistent questions and answered clearly: "No, I did not receive anything."

Then the man said, "OK. Leave here immediately. Pretend to go out for a walk with me, and then go straight back to Harbin."

"Immediately?"

"Yes, no time to waste."

"OK. I will get changed and put on my jacket."

"You don't need a jacket."

"It's an expensive English jacket tailored especially for me. I got it for dancing. Oh, I have an idea. Why don't we go to the dance hall this evening one last time, and then go to Harbin from there?"

"Don't be absurd. Your jacket or your life—which do you want? Besides, you were followed every time you went to the dance hall."

"Oh, I never noticed that."

"We never follow people in the manner carefree people like you would notice. Of course, it was fortunate that you are carefree. Anyway, hurry up. You have to leave now. I have already contacted the Harbin stationmaster."

The Harbin stationmaster warmly welcomed my father.

"I am glad to see you back safely. I know about your tribulations. Take leave and relax for a while. You can go back to Japan and later return with a wife.

"Now, apart from that, come to my home this evening. Let's drink and eat homemade dishes. My wife is a very good cook."

He then added gently, "You should thank that contact man with black glasses. He made a tremendous effort to take you back from the military."

After some time, a detached office was set up at the Harbin Railway Office per the order of the commander of the Kwantung Army.

This housed an underground special investigation unit under the Kwantung Army Field Railway Headquarters. Even at Mantetsu, only a select few top executives were informed of the existence of the office. It consisted of the members who were Japanese and Russian émigrés who had left Imperial Russia. The Japanese workers were given military status. Those who violated the requirements of the mission were court-martialed and punished accordingly.

At the end of the Second Sino-Japanese War, which coincided with the end of World War II, the Japanese who belonged to the detached office were treated the same as soldiers and were sent to Siberia to do forced labor under severe conditions. Most of them died. A small number did survive, but the question of their status arose. At issue was whether they should be treated as soldiers or civilians who belonged to Mantetsu.

It was only when this discussion occurred that the existence of the detached office, or the special investigative body, was revealed to the public.

Harbin

Saint Sophia Cathedral

Harbin is an exotic town with beautiful stone-paved streets. It is called "the town where Westerners live," or "Paris of the East."

It was once nothing more than a fishing village on the Songhua River. However, in 1989, when the Russian Empire constructed the Chinese Eastern Railway as a branch line of the Siberian Railway, it founded its base in Harbin.

Since then, the village developed rapidly as an important hub for railway and river transportation.

The town has much Western-style architecture including cathedrals of the Russian Orthodox Church such as Saint Nicholas Church and Saint Sophia Cathedral, and the prestigious Modern Hotel.

There were many aristocrats in exile living in the town who had evaded the Russian Revolution. Kitaiskaya Street, Harbin's main street, was proof of its international status with people from various countries milling about. At dusk, it was common for many people to go out for a walk.

When the bank of the Songhua River became faintly darkened by twilight, making it appear to be shrouded by light grey ink, an elderly Russian could be seen playing the balalaika.

My newlywed father and mother often took a walk on Kitaiskaya Street. My mother always had a strange feeling while walking. The previous few busy months seemed like a dream to her.

The image she had had of Manchuria was herself traveling a vast desert, occasionally finding a willow tree standing alone in the far distance, and a small mud house teetering on collapse. However, in reality, she felt as if she were in a Western city.

My mother had been learning homemaking while attending a sewing class when her sewing teacher suggested she to go to Manchuria and get married. The teacher had been asked by a distant relative who was a stationmaster in Mantetsu to find a bride for a young man with a promising future. She chose a smart girl—my mother.

"My father fell in love with Tomiko at first sight and they wasted no time getting married. The newlyweds returned to Harbin to meet the Stationmaster.

The Stationmaster, who was excited to see my mother, exclaimed "Oh, you have returned so early. I gave you special leave. Why didn't you take more time to relax in Japan?"

His wife said, smiling, "You have married such a pretty bride." Then, referring to my father's martial arts passion, she added, "Don't fight any more!"

My father replied, "I don't fight. Anyway, it would be futile for anyone to try to beat me!"

Everyone laughed.

"I understand you are in a foreign land for the first time. If you have any problems, don't hesitate. Just come and ask us for help," the Stationmaster's wife kindly said to the bride.

The home that my father arranged for their new life was an apartment where Russian people also lived. His idea was that living in Harbin was a special occasion, and it would be fun to become friends with Russians rather than living in a Japanese community at the apartment provided by Mantetsu.

The architecture of their apartment was elegant Art Nouveau style brick. They lived on the ground floor. Next door was a Russian aristocratic widow in exile.

On her first day, my mother went to her door to say hello. Her knocks were answered by a lady. Dressed in black from the top of her head to her toes, she cradled a white cat in her left arm. Its eyes were unusually glittery, making my mother step backward. The widow hurriedly released the cat into a back room.

The widow poured tea generously from a big samovar and welcomed her new neighbors. They quietly drank the tea in a relaxed manner by a pechka, an oven brought from Russia, sometimes exchanging smiles.

The Russians in exile had a farm in their neighborhood. Milk was delivered to the widow every morning. From that day, she always shared milk with my mother. It was freshly drawn, but my mother did not find it easy to drink raw milk. Even after she boiled it, drinking it took effort.

In return, she brought the widow Japanese sweets like *yokan*, sweet bean jelly, or *manju*, cakes filled with sweet bean paste. The borscht they cooked together was soft and tasty, different from a restaurant dish.

My mother remembered for the rest of her life that the first day she experienced snow in Harbin was the last day of August. It was like a small white petal, or the white floss of dandelions, that was falling from high up in the sky. It was a sign of the start of the snowy season.

Moreover, it was the first experience of snow on the continent for my mother.

"Wow, it's snowing!" she said excitedly.

She dashed out of the apartment. As she extended her kimono sleeves wide like a scarecrow, throwing up her hands, and spinning around in joy of being snowed on, the Russian aristocratic widow held her black umbrella over my mother's head quietly.

My mother got used to living in Harbin. The onion-like round roof of the cathedrals of the Russian Orthodox Church looked like freshly steamed tasty *manju* when she was happy, and like an onion when she was lonely, slightly irritating her eyes.

She spent the extremely cold, snowy winter protected by the double windows and soft warmth of her own pechka.

In the New Year, when lilac flowers bloomed, my mother was expecting to deliver her first baby in Harbin. She had thought of having her first childbirth at her parents' home in Japan, but that would take half a year including the time needed before and after the delivery.

The Stationmaster's wife had told my mother that she would come to help her anytime, but on that day, it was early morning, and my mother decided to go to hospital on her own. As she was trying to call a rickshaw at her apartment entrance, the Russian widow came out and called a horse wagon.

My mother was taken to hospital in a horse wagon driven by a Russian driver.

It was an easy delivery, but she entered the hospital early in the morning and the baby was born in the evening. A young nurse accompanied her throughout the day. The nurse displayed a pretty dimple when she smiled. She said it was her fist time to attend a birthing. She and my mother were very excited and tearfully shared the joy together.

On the day she was released, the young nurse said she hoped to have such a pretty baby herself someday, and carried the baby in her arms to see my mother off at the entrance.

When the rickshaw arrived at my mother's home and she got out, the Russian widow took the baby from my mother in silence, and slowly walked up the steps of the entrance.

Life in Harbin, sharing heartfelt communication beyond any language barrier, made my mother into a generous-hearted international woman.

When his first daughter was born in Harbin, my father was a little disappointed to hear that it was a girl. He regretfully said to people, "Because I was out for some time, the baby came out a girl," as if the baby would have been a boy if he had been at home but somehow transformed into a girl because he happened to be away on a business trip.

However, he started to think that a girl was okay for the first baby.

"People say 'Have a girl first and a boy next,' don't they? After a girl, a boy who will be my heir will appear. His older sister will take care of him," he said to himself, helping him accept the fact.

Above all, the joy of becoming a father was tremendous. Having his own child, a baby who resembled him, was a happiness greater than anything else he had experienced in his life. He went everywhere proudly cradling this pretty baby girl.

On the days after his night shifts, he took her to the Mantetsu Judo club.

He wore a *shirogasuri*, a white kimono adorned with black splash patterns, which my mother had tailored for him, and put on a *hakama*, a formal pleated and divided skirt, over it. He tied his folded judo uniform to one end of his black belt, hung it over his shoulder, and went out holding his baby with her belly facing up in the other arm.

He looked like a student holding a baby instead of books. His judo uniform at the end of his black belt swung on his back to the rhythm of his long stride.

At his dojo, his colleagues had been waiting for his newborn. They were all single men so it was rare for them to see a baby. Ignoring judo practice, and dropping their typical tough-guy personas, they played peekaboo and held the baby in turns. She kept smiling without showing any sign of fear.

The men got a little careless one day.

Judo members always took a bath after practice. On that day, the big boys stood in a circle in the bathtub and passed the baby wrapped in a towel from hand to hand. At first the men were passing the baby very carefully, but gradually as the game gained speed, the men passed the baby in a rhythmic manner as if she were a volleyball. The baby was strong; she kept smiling in everyone's arms, holding her own cherry-pink colored tiny fingers. My father felt proud to be a father of such a cute baby.

When the baby made it back to my father, his glasses were fogged with steam. The baby slipped from my father's arms into the hot bath.

"Nooo!" the men screamed, and the baby was immediately snatched safely out of the hot water.

When my mother was informed of the incident and arrived, the baby was sound asleep as if nothing had happened to her.

One day, my mother said that the milk the Russian aristocratic widow living next door gave her every day was too much to drink. On hearing this my father said, "Yes, a milk bath. Bring me milk. Yang Guifei used a perfume bath, but here, we will give her a milk bath and make her the most beautiful baby in the world!" He then skillfully bathed the baby in a washtub filled with milk.

My mother had been making great effort to drink all the milk she was given, but since that day, she stopped drinking it to save as much as possible for the milk bath. At dusk, my father and mother held their baby while walking on Kitaiskaya Street.

With the start of the Marco Polo Bridge Incident, my father was ordered to go to Fengtai, and my mother decided to go to Dalian and wait for him. On the day of departure, the Russian widow next door held my mother with her baby in her arms, and gently said in Russian, *"Do svidanya*—goodbye, best wishes." Parting was painful.

The Marco Polo Bridge Incident

Marco Polo Bridge

It happened on July 7th, 1937.

A single gunshot fired near the Marco Polo Bridge in the southern suburb of Beijing prompted more gunfire from both the Japanese and the Chinese armies. Soon the fighting spread throughout the continent like a wildfire racing across dried plains that keeps burning farther and wider.

Even if it was true that the Japanese army and the 29th Route Army under Song Zheyuan, both stationed in Fengtai, had been on alert regarding the actions of each other, who could have imagined that the single gunshot on that night would start the Sino-Japanese War, a war that would last for eight long years?

The Marco Polo Bridge is a magnificent stone bridge over the Yongding River, 20 kilometers southwest of Beiping. Elaborately carved lions adorn each handrail of the 235 meter-bridge. It is also known as a scenic spot for moon viewing. At the foot of the bridge is a stone tablet which reads "Morning Moon over Lugou," the calligraphy done by the Qianlong Emperor of the Qing dynasty.

However, on that night, the moon was not visible.

Who fired the first shot toward the sky on the night of the Star Festival? If it had been a bright moonlit night, the truth might have been illuminated under the moon with nowhere to hide. However, to this day, it has been veiled in the deep dark sky of that night.

At that time, the Japanese government and the general headquarters of the military were in a panic wondering if the shot came from the local Japanese military division stationed there, but my father denied that possibility completely, insisting, "It was not a conspiracy concocted by the Japanese side."

My father had worked at Fengtai Station close to the Marco Polo Bridge at the time of the Langfang Incident two years before, and learned the situations of both the Japanese and the Chinese armies. According to what he told me later, the local conditions at that time did not allow either side to initiate an attack.

Of course, their relationship was strained to the breaking point, but the first attacker would be the loser, and each side could not make the first move even if they wanted to. Under such an extremely strained air felt by both Japan and China, it is even possible that a third party was the culprit.

The Marco Polo Bridge Incident

This theory about a third party instigator has been raised lately.

While the Japanese army was astonished and panicked at that gunshot, the Chinese Communist Party issued telegrams encouraging war against Japan with extraordinary speed on the following day, as if they had already known about the incident in advance.

In any case, considering the series of various incidents that had been occurring in large or small scale between the two countries since the Manchurian Incident, the conflict could not be avoided with or without the occurrence of the Star Festival gunshot.

At first, the incident seemed to be local.

But, however small the first spark was, once fire started spreading, it would not be extinguished so easily. Moreover, if a gust of wind stirred it, the fire would soon get out of control.

At first, the Japanese government and the general headquarters of the military had a policy of seeing it as "an incident of no expansion to be solved locally."

General Kanji Ishiwara was against the view that the incident would spread. His opinion was that they should consider the Manchuria and Northern China regions separately. However, there were elements who wished to take this conflict as an opportunity to solve the geopolitical problems between Japan and China with military force.

After all, the Japanese Konoe cabinet accepted the request made by the Ministry of the Army and the General Staff Office, and decided to deploy three divisions of troops from Japan, the Kwantung Army, and troops of the Japanese Korean Army.

It was only a deployment "for the purpose of protecting Japanese residents" while the policy of non-expansion was maintained. But the staff of the Japanese Garrison headquarters in Tianjin clearly took the situation as "Now is a golden opportunity to solve the problem between Japan and China."

A cease-fire agreement was reached at one point, but on July 25th, 1937, a confrontation between the Japanese and the Chinese armies near Langfang, a city between Beiping and Tianjin, intensified the fighting. Soon, a serious war spread throughout the continent.

The Chinese Communist Party made rapid advances on the day after the incident as if it had been planned. Also, Chiang Kai-shek clearly displayed animosity toward Japan.

On July 28th, the Japanese army advanced into the Northern China battle front.

In August, under Lieutenant-General Hideki Tojo, Chief of Staff of the Kwangtung Army, two brigades of the Kwangtung Army advanced over the Great Wall into the Chahar Province. The frontline of the war was military transport. On receiving the order by the Imperial Army, troops and war supplies were transported from Manchuria by Mantetsu workers, and from Japan by Ministry of Railways workers.

Then, as the war expanded from local to wider areas on the continent, many Mantetsu workers were dispatched to the Northern China Railway Office to work for military transport. The number of workers again increased later, and the Northern China Railway Office became independent from Mantetsu to form Kahoku Traffic Co., Ltd., and continued to develop as a subsidiary of Mantetsu.

Due to the expansion of the incident, my father was sent to the Northern China Railway Office and assigned to work for military transport at Fengtai Station. It was extremely difficult to recover the railroad that had been cut off and repair the destroyed bridge.

On August 20th, Fengtai Transport Team was launched to maintain the Jingsui and Jinghan lines. The 20 passenger cars left at the station were used as the office.

My father was working at the Fengtai Station again two years after he had left. He nostalgically looked around the station yard thinking, "I never expected to come back to Fengtai Station so soon."

His first appointment there was at the time of the Langfang Incident. He was reminiscing about the time when he had infiltrated the village disguised as a Chinese citizen and met his contact with black glasses. Then he was sent to Zhangjiakou in Chahar Province.

On the way from Beijing to Chahar Province, an Inner Mongolia Autonomous Region, the train passed Nankou Station 30 kilometers outside Beijing at the foot of the Great Wall, climbed the 33% grade Nankou Pass to Badaling, then chugged through a tunnel before descending on a 25% downhill grade to Kangzhuang. The train was operated in switchback mode on these steep mountains between Nankou and Kangzhuang, with locomotives attached to the front and the back of the train.

After passing this difficult section, the view from the train suddenly opened to vast ochre-colored plains. While passengers were spellbound by the scenery of the tremendous wasteland that unfolded before their eyes, the train entered the Mengjiang area.

Zhangjiakou Railway Office

Dajingmen

On June 20th, 1938, a railway office opened in Zhangjiakou. At the same time, railway offices were opened in Beijing, Tianjing, and Jinan.

Then on April 17th, 1939, with the Mantetsu Northern China Office as its parent company, Kahoku Traffic Co., Ltd. was founded. One of the company mottoes was "We shall achieve the mission of transportation on the continent."

Kahoku Traffic Co., Ltd. assumed the tasks of maintenance, operation, and development of the massive number and variety of railway transportation options in the Mengjiang region of Northern China.

After serving as a vehicle allocation commander at the allocation section of the transportation division with the launch of the Zhangjiakou Railway Office, by November 1938 my father had already assumed office as the chief assistant stationmaster of Zhangjiakou Station.

Zhangjiakou is located 200 kilometers northwest of Beijing, the biggest city along the outer Great Wall, at the entrance to the Mongolian desert. It is where Chinese and Mongolian civilizations meet.

This city is an important base leading to Outer Mongolia with a fortress that used to cover the entire northern area. At Dajingmen, the gateway to the Great Wall, there is an inscription that reads "Dahaoheshan" meaning "beautiful rivers and mountains."

This city is known as a trading spot for Inner and Outer Mongolia, where wool, sheep skin, salt and other goods from inner Mongolia are bought and sold. The area around Dajingmen is the center of trade.

The evening sun in Zhangjiakou was beautiful.

In the direction of the setting sun, a caravan of camels, loaded with baggage hanging on both sides of their backs, was sometimes seen. They would amble slowly, their bells clattering outside of the gate of Dajingmen.

Zhangjiakou was also an important point for transportation.

It was the center of seven streets, including Jingchang Street leading to Beijing, Zhangku Street leading to Mongolia's Ulan Bator (Kulun), and Changduo Street leading to Duolun. It was called a "land port" and flourished as the center of transportation and commerce.

The city was surrounded by the mountains of the Mongolian plateau in three directions, and on the mountain to the north, a branch of the

Zhangjiakou Railway Office

Great Wall twisting here and there was visible.

The Qingshui River was flowing narrowly north to south through the center of the town, with neighboring towns developed on both sides.

In early spring, the Mongolian wind scooped up and blew yellow dust. The yellow dust formed clouds that covered the sky and darkened the town. The residents could not open their eyes when this stinging yellow sand flew in the air.

After the Mongolian wind passed, fresh green buds appeared all at once. Apricot flowers and Mongolian cherry blossoms grew in full bloom.

In summertime, cool evening breezes blew like those on highlands and large sunflowers bloomed.

In mid-fall, the sky displayed a perfectly clear blue.

Winter came early, and was extremely cold. After the surface of Quingshui River froze, children skated on it. But the north wind blew violently. The frigid air froze people to their bones.

After the Marco Polo Bridge Incident, Hideki Tojo, Chief of Staff of the Kuwantang Army, conducted Operation Chahar and one of the brigades, the Honda Brigade, entered Zhangjiakou on August 27th, then Datong on September 13th, and finally Pingdiquan on September 24th, occupying and securing important bases along the Jingbao railway line one after another.

Then the 26th Division was formed. Under the command of Lieutenant General Jun Ushirogu, it occupied Suiyuan on October 14th, and Baotou on October 17th. Suiyuan and Baotou had been the bases for the Chinese troops of Fu Zuoyi, but they had been chased away to Wuyuan, the westernmost town of Inner Mongolia.

In January 1938, the Japanese imperial military headquarters in Mongolia opened in Zhangjiakou. Lieutenant General Shigeru Hasunuma assumed command.

Then in March, the headquarters of the second independent mixed brigade was deployed in Zhangjiakou, the 26th division in Datong, and a cavalry brigade in Baotou.

The imperial military headquarters in Mongolia and the headquarters of the military police, the kempei-tai, were stationed in Zhangjiakou, and many military officers could be seen at the station.

One kempei from headquarters had received five jute bags with opium that had been sent from Salaqi at Zhangjiakou Station, and spent the money to pay his mistress and enjoy lavish meals at restaurants.

Such behavior was becoming all too common. Even though he was an officer, his illicit sale of opium could not be ignored.

The stationmaster accused the officer, who was the second son of a viscount. The officer exclaimed, "You are impertinent!" and slapped the stationmaster's cheek. But he did not truly grasp who was being impertinent.

The stationmaster held his own head and cried.

The kempei superintendent came to offer his sincere apology, asking the stationmaster to forgive what the officer had done. Still, as a result, the stationmaster was reassigned to a station far inland. He indirectly asked my father to go with him, but my father could not leave Zhangjiakou at that time.

My father's work as the chief assistant stationmaster was of course important, but moreover, he was teaching judo to the Zhangjiakou kempei. When he had been transferred to the railway office of Zhangjiakou, he immediately recruited practitioners, started a judo club, and began practicing intensively.

One day, the chief of the military police himself came and asked my father to teach judo to the kempei. He said he strongly desired to have instruction that had been endorsed by judo master Sanpo Toku.

The kempei of the Empire of Japan were worthy of the name. Their attitude toward judo practice was very enthusiastic. They endured my father's strict instruction that was even beyond their own enthusiasm and developed the skill to become dan rank holders one after another.

One of these kempei was Miyamoto. He was especially enthusiastic. After practice he followed my father home out of adoration. The first thing he did after arriving at my father's home was to lift my father's daughter, saying she was so cute.

"Isn't she beautiful? She was polished in milk baths in Harbin," my father always said proudly.

"When she was born, I happened to be away on business and she was born a girl. But we are expecting a boy soon. Yes, absolutely a boy. Definitely a boy."

Hearing my father talking happily, my mother hoped to have a boy next.

Repeatedly being told that the baby would be a boy, my mother grew to think that the next baby would be a boy. The power of the baby kicking inside herself felt strong, changing her hope into conviction that the baby was surely a boy.

My father was very motivated. He proudly said to Miyamoto that he was sure that they were expecting a boy, so soon thereafter Miyamoto brought him a high quality military blanket as a gift.

While playing with the baby girl, Miyamoto kept saying "I envy you, I want a child myself. I want a boy who will be my heir."

Miyamoto had always been longing for a warm family of his own. He had lost his father when he was small.

This man of the Military Police had dignified looks, a strict attitude toward military tasks, and no mercy. His iron-hearted personality frightened everyone. But Miyamoto seemed to let down his guard when he was with my father.

One day, my father and Miyamoto were on the same train from Baotou to Beijing on duty. Miyamoto seemed to have had followed a marauding band of the Chinese Eighth Route Army; he was exhausted and lost in sleep beside my father.

In the far back seat of the passengers' car, there was a woman holding a large lump, a baby wrapped in a coat. The woman looked somewhat strange, as if she was frightened or enduring a tribulation in an agitated state.

My father wondered if the baby in her arms was ill and he grew worried.

When he approached her, her face strained with terror, and shook her head as if refusing.

"What's the matter? Is your baby …" before my father finished, Miyamoto leapt to his side in an instant. Miyamoto took the baby in the coat suddenly and said to the woman, "Please follow me," and headed to the staff room.

In the staff room, Miyamoto took the baby from the woman and let the baby lie on the desk belly up. It was too big to be an infant. He looked to be two, but to my father, the baby's age did not really matter.

What mattered to him was the face. It was gruesome. It looked to have been strongly compressed by an enormous power; it was like a shrunken balloon. The eyes, the nose, and the mouth were crooked and squished to the center, the color of rotten winter melon.

The baby was dead. The body smelled foul, suggesting that the child had died not recently.

Miyamoto started to unstrap the flowery-patterned baby coat. The woman who had been pale and shivering suddenly started crying out, "Please forgive me, please, please forgive me..." and madly held onto Miyamoto's arm.

"Shut up! Get your hands off me!" he cried, pushing the woman away.

He then violently opened the front of the baby coat.

"Oh, no..." the woman shrieked in desperation.

The belly of the dead child was swollen abnormally, and along the center was a sloppily stitched seam.

This was something he could have expected, but he could no longer see it. My father bit his lower lip so hard it bled, and he could not move. He was overwhelmed with anger.

"Why did she do this?" he wondered.

He wanted to immediately bolt out of the small room which suddenly was fraught with unbearable tension.

He pressed his forehead to the window and forced himself to look outside. However, what he saw out the window, in the darkness, was the same grotesque scene. Under the dim yellow light, reflections of the fearful faces of three people in total silence were reflected, as if the scene was chasing the train, and the speeding train was unable to distance itself from this macabre drama.

The train kept running across the vast plains throughout the night.

My father had never experienced anything as sad and forlorn as the clanking train wheels that night. Until that night, the familiar sound of the train wheels were as familiar and as pleasant as his own heartbeat.

The woman had stopped speaking or crying, but was just crouching low and shivering. Only her eyes showed her hatred, glowing ominously.

The train kept running at full speed.

While wishing only to reach the next station, he felt as if the train would never stop, running for eternity to the end of the land, to the end of the world.

That would be fine. That might be better. That would save this mother and her child.

The next day, Miyamoto came to my father to tell him the details.

"I was so surprised at that incident. I have witnessed cases of illicit selling and smuggling of opium many times, but this case was extraordinary even to me."

The crackdown on the illicit sale and smuggling of opium had been severe, but the smugglers outsmarted the police by continuously finding new ways. It was a never-ending game of wits between those who were chasing and those being chased.

Sometimes opium was hidden in the body of a shamisen, in the hollows of a *go* board, or inside a whole roasted chicken in place of a kidney. But even a devil could not have conceived of hiding it in a dead child's body.

What was a relief in this case was that the child was not killed for this purpose.

The mother refused to leave her child who had died of illness, and she was told that she could stay with him longer if she agreed to go to Beijing.

The one who suggested the idea was the father of the child. He had been waiting for their arrival in Beijing to receive opium, but he insisted that he did not know the mother and dead child, not to mention of opium.

"What kind of father is he? And the child was a boy…" my father sighed deeply.

Train drivers and conductors were often asked to secretly carry opium. These railroad employees were in the best position to help criminals intent on smuggling. A space under the assistant's locomotive seat or the corner of the conductor's room were the safest places to hide opium. The crew on night cargo trains seemed to have been asked often.

There was great incentive for those who were asked. Employing minimal caution would result in good food and money that was far greater than their salary. Once they were involved, they could not stop. In fact, they were not allowed to refuse.

My father was approached in that way too.

Once, a train passenger treated my father to a big feast in Beijing.

The next day, the passenger came to my father's apartment to ask him to deliver a very important item to the passenger's friend who had been at the feast the night before.

My mother immediately sensed the scam and said, "My husband pays no attention to anything else once he is on duty. He often leaves things behind, so we cannot ask him to do anything important when he is on duty."

The man could see that my mother had guessed his intention. He gave up and left.

A neighbor who worked as a train conductor in the same company had agreed to the same request. Later, he was arrested for delivering opium and put in prison. His wife and two children had to wait for him to serve his two-year sentence.

When my mother told Miyamoto, he explained, "Ah, their father will never come back. He probably died a long time ago."

When the transporters for smuggled opium were captured, they were sent to Sinuiju. The prisoners there lived in such severe conditions that most died before completing their sentences. My mother had heard such rumors.

"Oh, the rumors are true, after all," my mother said.

But what Miyamoto had said was actually a bit different from the rumor.

Those who had been arrested were sent to Sinuiju, but in the middle of the journey they were pushed out of the train into the Yalu River on the border between Manchuria and North Korea. The Yalu is a great river of about 795 kilometers originating in Mount Paektu of the Changbai Mountains and flowing into the Yellow River.

Before reaching Sinuiju, those arrested were eliminated. If they were investigated, they might leak some inconvenient information. If a spilled secret unveiled further secrets, the Imperial Army would be unavoidably involved. Not only the army, but the government, the police and all such organizations were run on funds gotten from the opium trade. Besides, those arrested were nobodies after all. No one protested when they were pushed out of the train to perish in the Yalu River. Rather, the ones who pushed the prisoners to their deaths were appreciated for saving others who had been involved.

However, they had to provide the family of the arrested with some reasonable explanation. First, they notified the family that the term was two or three years depending on the charge. Then when the supposed term was about to end, they notified the death to the family with a believable explanation such as death from suicide or illness due to the awful prison conditions.

After some time, a death notice was delivered to the mother and two children who had been waiting anxiously for their husband and father.

The father of the boy who had opium packed into his gut and delivered by the train from Baotou to Beijing steadfastly denied the accusation, and even denied being the boy's father. This totally disgusted the investigator. Naturally enough, the father was sent on the train over the Yalu River.

The mother who had clung to her dead son succumbed to mental illness and was hospitalized.

The Great Badaling Flood

The section between Juyong Pass and Sanbao (Jingbao line) that turned into a vast riverbed

On May 12th, 1939, when the troubles of the Mengjiang region were starting to settle, a conflict between the Japanese and the Soviet armies occurred at the border of Manchuria and Outer Mongolia.

It was the start of the Battles of Khalkhin Gol.

In this time of turmoil, my father's long-awaited second child was about to be born. My father was beside himself. He told his wife to call him again and again when the baby was born before he left home for work.

The nurse who attended the delivery of my mother's second child was, by coincidence, the same nurse with pretty dimples on her cheeks who had assisted the delivery of her first baby in Harbin.

"What a curious turn of fate," they said, and were happy to see each other again. The young nurse introduced herself again giving her name *Naoko Hoshino*. Naoko, who had been a novice nurse, had now become a full-fledged nurse.

When the Marco Polo Bridge Incident occurred and the Japanese army advanced past the Great Wall, some medical staff including doctors and nurses moved to Zhangjiakou with the army. Naoko was one such nurse.

My mother and Naoko quickly hit it off and became good friends.

My mother gave a birth to a baby, a girl. It was me, their second daughter.

My father had been longing for a boy and was convinced his dream would come true this time. I can imagine how this news disappointed him.

I can also guess that a girl was not what my mother had expected. But she thought that a boy's life and a girl's life were equally precious, and gave me the name *Sachiko*, a child of happiness, wishing me a happy life.

My father recovered from his deep disappointment. He told himself, "Now a girl has been born, and a girl is pretty. The next time will be a boy. The third time will be the charm." Convincing himself thusly, he postponed his wish.

Later, my father encouraged my mother to visit her parents to celebrate my 100th day. My mother was happy to go back to Japan for the first time with her daughters in both arms.

Naoko came to see her at home occasionally after she left hospital,

The Great Badaling Flood

and held the baby and her older sister who had been born in Harbin, saying they were cute and loving them as if they were her own sisters.

However, at that time, on July 25th, 1939, a once-in-a-century heavy rain hit the Mengjiang region of northern China.

Floods hit the area from Kangzhuang in Chahar Province to Badaling of the Great Wall, 4,000 meters above sea level. Landslides occurred in Qinglongqiao. The railway tracks between Qinglongqiao and Nankou were washed away. All railway facilities were devastated.

The sleepers were buried in mud, and the rails were twisted like candy canes.

The mountains in this area were high and steep with Badaling the highest. They were covered with rocks and no tall trees. But bushes grew in places, and some weeds were attached to the surface of the rocks. The rainwater rushed down without soaking into the soil. The rain on that day fell with tremendous force and caused a devastating landslide. Heavy rain became the gushing mud that carried the rails away completely.

It grew dark. The roaring rainfall even smothered conversations.

The train on the Jingbao line from Beijing stopped at Qinglongqiao Station and could not continue.

(Beijing – Nankou – Juyongguan – Qinglongqiao – Xibozi – Kangzhuang – Huailai – Xiahuayuan – Xuanhua – Zhangjiakou)

On this train, Director-General Sonyu Otani and Vice Director-General Yamanishi of North China Development Company were traveling together.

After the Marco Polo Bridge Incident, as Japan advanced into northern China, the Northern China Development Company was established to play the role of giving general guidance on matters regarding the economy and industry in the Mengjiang region of northern China. It was a company of Japanese national policy concern.

Sonyu Otani was its first director-general. He had attended a ceremony to celebrate the establishment of the Kahoku Traffic Co., Ltd. as a guest.

At this time, on July 26th of the same year, he was traveling from Beijing to Zhangjiakou to attend the general meeting to be held at Longyian Mining Co., Ltd.

This company was founded for the purpose of mining, supplying and selling iron ore, with great expectations to develop the Mengjiang region.

Director-General Otani and his party took shelter in a railroad maintenance house, and changed vehicles to reach Kangzhuang by the cars that had come to rescue them. But further down the road, they did not have any choice other than walking to Huailai in the pouring rain.

They managed to arrive in Zhangjiakou, but Director Otani was totally exhausted. Two days later, he died of an unknown illness at a Japanese hotel in front of the station.

Sonyu Otani served as Minister of Colonial Affairs in the first cabinet of Prime Minister Konoe.

He was born as the younger brother of Kozui Otani, the 22nd head of Nishi Honganji Temple. The poet Takeko Kujo was his older sister.

Kozui Otani was recorded in history not only as the head of Nishi Honganji, but also as the explorer who organized the "Otani expedition" to a series of Silk Road sites in the early 20th century.

Sonyu Otani unexpectedly had his life end in Mengjiang on the Asian land where his brother Kozui Otani had put his heart and soul into his expedition. I feel some kind of wonder, as if there was a connection between "blood and land" somewhere deep in that vast space.

In any case, in 1939, the downpours that hit the Mengjiang region of northern China continued for nearly one month, halting train operations between Beijing and Zhangjiakou.

In those days, many Japanese had moved to China seeking a job.

The Mengjiang region was the land of hope second only to Manchuria, with companies such as Kahoku Traffic, North China Development, and the newly founded Longyian Mining. In addition, it was home to resources that included Datong Coal Mine and the ironstones in the Yin Mountains. These opportunities prompted Japanese to move into the region.

However, the flood kept people in Beijing. Even in such circumstances, people could not stay in Beijing for a long time. Many people walked to Badaling from Nankou along the sleepers buried in mud and the rails twisted by the flood.

The suspension of railway services greatly affected not just travelers but food transportation as well. Food and materials were not delivered from Beijing to the Zhangjiakou region for more than one month.

The Great Badaling Flood

Immediately after the flood, the military officers, workers from Kahoku Traffic and its related companies, and more than 20,000 laborers, gathered to jointly labor on the recovery work day and night.

Not just the rails, but the telegraph poles were washed away as well, cutting off telephone lines. Here, carrier-pigeons were used for communication. These birds carried telegraphs more than a dozen times a day between the recovery sites and the supervisors.

Around this time, my father had planned to arrange for my mother, my older sister and me to return to Japan's mainland to celebrate my 100th day since birth. However, the rare once-in-a-century great flood cut off the railroad. With special arrangements provided by the military, we were flown from Zhangjiakou to Beijing in a military plane. However, it was a small plane that could carry only my mother and her daughters, not my father.

"It is my pleasure to fly with a young lady," the military officer gently said to my mother who was nervous.

"Oh, she is just a small girl who is still wearing a diaper." My father completely missed the fact it was actually a compliment paid to his wife.

The military plane flew into the vast blue sky to Beijing, and over the glowing mountains of the Great Wall that was winding like an enormous snake.

My sister was beside my mother while I was firmly held on my mother's lap.

On that day, fewer than 100 days after my birth, that flight set the record of the youngest Japanese to fly over the Great Wall in a Japanese military plane. This record will never be broken because a Japanese military plane will never again fly over the Great Wall.

After seeing the plane take off, my father took an alternate route from the group of Director-General Otani. The train was stopped at Kangzhuang. Since the train could not continue on its route, my father got off there, hired a Chinese guide who agreed to carry his travel bag, and walked up the 33 degree mountain road along the railroad.

By the time he passed Xibozi, it had already passed six in the evening.

On the route further ahead, rails and sleepers that had been washed away appeared. The road itself was unrecognizable. He reached a point where he saw a tunnel with a large opening 6 or 7 meters tall. There he faced a challenge. He had to cross a log bridge of nearly 4 meters.

As he looked back, he saw his guide take the bag off of his back, kneel down, and start to tremble. My father asked him what the matter was, but the guide kept trembling and pointed downward.

He saw a row of camels far down looking like ants. It was seemed like a bottomless ravine.

In addition, the guide said wolves prowled that area after it got dark so he begged my father to let him go home. My father balked at the possibility of his guide bailing out at this stage of the journey.

But the guide remained on his knees, clasping his palms over his head as if in prayer, touching his forehead onto the ground while repeatedly asking my father in tears to be released. Surely, the guide said, wolves inside the tunnel would gobble their entire bodies, not even leaving behind their bones.

With no other choice, my father decided to continue his journey on his own.

He crossed the bridge with clenched teeth. A wrong step would bring him straight down into the bowels of the ravine. Even after crossing the bridge, his knees kept trembling for some time.

Then he resolutely took out a shirt from his bag, rolled it, set it on fire, and threw it into the tunnel with all of his might. He paused for a moment to listen for strange sounds from inside the tunnel. Nothing.

By the evening of the following day, he could finally join his wife and children in Beijing.

After seeing his family safe in Beijing before their trip to Japan, he again went to Badaling which had become the muddy graveyard of sleepers and rails. Soon after he finally returned to Zhangjiakou.

The railway recovery work after the great flood was extremely difficult.

The construction had been expected to take at least a few months, but 20,000 workers from the military, Kahoku Traffic, and railway staff survived by cooking *mantou,* Chinese steamed buns, with steam produced by the grounded locomotives. Thanks to their great effort, the recovery was completed at an amazing speed. On August 21st, the trains started running again.

The Battle of Wuyuan

Wuyuan District

On December 20th, 1939, Fu Zuoyi's troops who had been stationed in Wuyuan abruptly attacked the town of Baotou. The Japanese army serving as guards were taken unprepared which led to many casualties in the ensuing battle.

Baotou was the terminal station of the Jingbao line (Beijing – Baotou).

Immediately south of Baotou was the great Yellow River flowing majestically despite having witnessed eons of bloodshed. This muddy river was so wide that the opposite side is often obscured due to the great distance.

It was the entrance to the Hexi Corridor of the Northern Silk Road that led to Mongolia along the Yellow River and the Uyghur region, a trade base for the entire northwestern region, and an important international trade center in the Mengjiang region. It was also a collection center for sheep skin and wool; there were long rows of caravans of camels.

Baotou means "the place where deer live."

At the time of the Marco Polo Bridge Incident, the Japanese military invaded and occupied Baotou. Fu Zuoyi's troops fled Suiyuan and Baotou where they had been stationed, and were driven to Wuyuan, far to the west.

On September 1st, 1939, the Chanan Government (Zhangjiakou), Jinbei Government (Datong), and Autonomous Government of Mengjiang Federation (Suiyuan) were merged to form the Mengjiang United Autonomous Government with Zhangjiakou as its capital.

The chairman of the state was Prince De, the vice-Chairmen were Xia Gong and Yu Pinqing, the general army commander was Li Shouxin, and the supreme advisor was Shoji Kanai.

The Japanese army had placed its cavalry headquarters in Baotou. Unrest in the Mengjiang region had improved.

However, during the season when the Yellow River froze, the enemy started attacking from the south riverbank. Eventually, Fu Zuoyi's rebels made a daring raid.

The cavalry headquarters was completely disgraced.

The Japanese army decided to wait for the New Year before carrying out Operation Wuyuan on January 15, 1940.

Commands were given immediately to the Mengjiang government's traffic department to improve the road between Baotou and Wuyuan, to build bridges in the creek area, and to accompany the military advancement. It was a wet area with moats. However, most bridges had been destroyed by Fu Zuoyi's rebel army. The repair work was extremely difficult during a winter that saw temperatures drop all the way to 30 degrees centigrade below zero (-22F). The reality was actually far worse due to a north wind that blew ferociously.

The strategy of this operation was to travel in cars rather than as a cavalry unit. About one thousand cars were recruited from the military's motorized unit, more from Mengjiang automobile company, and from other sources as well.

Thus, the cavalry had been transformed into a motorized unit. The soldiers were assigned to ride in roofless cargo trucks, and advanced into the wetlands amid a strong wind blowing dust. The Yin Mountains stood to the north.

On this occasion, my father was assigned to take part in Operation Wuyuan as the Salaqi Stationmaster of Suiyuan Province and the railway team leader. His task was to help with the railway transportation of support materials.

Also, in the Salaqi area, he supported the battle between the Chinese Eighth Route Army and Japan's Yamasaki's unit, and worked aiding offensive operations.

The Salaqi area was the roughest area on the Jinbao railway line. The Eighth Route Army and marauding bands frequently attacked with sniper shots and explosions. They would cut off or destroy railways, attack and destroy trains, and burn down station buildings.

The great Yin Mountains continued to the north, and the Yellow River flowed vibrantly to the south; the area across the river was the most suitable camp for marauding bands. In particular, the mounted bandits led by the infamous Ma Zhanshan often operated in this area.

Ma Zhanshan was from Jilin Province of Manchuria. When Manchukuo was established, he at once submitted to the Japanese army, and assumed the position of the first military commander-in-chief of Manchukuo. Later, however, he ran away. His whereabouts remained unknown until he resurfaced on this land of Mengjiang where he had formed the Northeastern Advance Force to fight the Japanese army.

Kahoku Traffic formed a "Railway Team" to maintain the railway security of Jinbao Railway from Houhe (Suiyuan) to Baotou, and protect residents along the unsafe areas of the railroad. They worked with locals to ensure stability and pacification.

The stationmaster also served as the leader of the railway team.

According to a report written by a spy, Fu Zuoyi had ordered Ma Zhanshan to destroy the railroad between Baotou and Houhe (Suiyuan) again during the Battle of Wuyuan. The target was Salaqi Station, the very station my father was serving at.

At Salaqi Station, the stationmaster and all the staff united in determination to protect the station.

The Japanese 26th Division and the troops led by Seishiro Itagaki fought against Fu Zuoyi's army. They drove 20,000 rebels of the regular army as far as the Ningxian Province border.

Wuyuan was the only grain-producing area of Ningxian Province, located 250 kilometers west of Baotou, the westernmost region of Inner Mongolia. The land was expansive and fertile, with good water supplies, suitable for agriculture and farming. Fu Zuoyi's troops were desperate to keep control of the land at all cost.

Meanwhile, for the Japanese army, the Wuyuan area was the front line of their protection, but Naosaburo Okabe, Commander-in-Chief of the Mongolia Garrison Army, said, "The purpose of Operation Wuyuan is to defeat Fu Zuoyi's rebels and destroy their base around Wuyuan. We will not occupy the land. Once we achieve our goal, we will withdraw at an appropriate time."

However, Shinichi Tanaka, Staff Chief of the Mongolia Garrison Army, did not consider this ideal, and decided he would station police to guard the Wuyuan region after the operation was completed and the army left.

Accordingly, for the implementation unit of Operation Wuyuan, Lieutenant Colonel Koichiro Kuwahara, Commander-in-Chief of Special Service Agency, was appointed the General Commander-in-Chief. Officers of the Special Service Agency and 1,200 Japanese soldiers were recruited from among policemen in Japan by the security division chief of the Mengjiang United Autonomous Government. Together with 500

The Battle of Wuyuan

soldiers of the Inner Mongolian Army, they constituted the governmental complex forces for Wuyuan.

However, the poorly equipped former policemen who had been hastily thrown together were counterattacked by 20,000 rebels led by Fu Zuoyi. The battle resumed in Wuyuan.

The Japanese Air Force urgently joined as reinforcements, but additional ground troops were slowed by thick mud created by melting snow and rebel attacks, delaying their arrival. Former Chinese soldiers working for the Japanese military betrayed the Japanese.

On March 20th, 1940, Wuyuan was totally in enemy hands. Defeat was complete.

Lieutenant Colonel Koichiro Kuwahara had been fighting on a rooftop when an enemy bullet tore through his belly, ending the life of a key Japanese military figure.

Assistant Commander Ichinosuke Shinohara fought valiantly, but in a storm of enemy bullets, he capitulated. To die honorably, he committed harakiri, ritual suicide, by slashing his own belly horizontally. While samurai often had someone then behead them, Shinohara finished off his own life by putting a bullet through his head.

Ichinosuke Shinohara had joined the May 15 Incident, the 1932 attempted coup d'état in Japan. A group of 11 naval officers assassinated Prime Minister Tsuyoshi Inukai. After completing a light four-year prison term, he moved to Manchuria and joined Junnosuke Date's mounted bandits for some time before participating in the assault on Wuyuan with the Special Service Agency in Baotou.

Ichinosuke Shinohara wrote lyrics for the song of the Baotou Special Service Agency.

> *Under a spell of extreme heartlessness and coldness,*
> *Through the deep clouds of dust and the north wind,*
> *We advance paving our way*
> *To the frontline of our operation.*
> *We are the Great Baotou Agency with burning spirits...*

Although the exact number is uncertain, the Battle of Wuyuan caused the deaths and injuries of over 100 men and dozens of Japanese policemen. These policemen who were recruited urgently in Japan died on the frozen tundra one after another without even knowing where they were or even that Wuyuan was in the Mengjiang region. In fact, they didn't even know who they were fighting against or why.

The motorized unit members who had managed to survive had their vehicle engines damaged due to the north wind and mud. The bridges had been destroyed by the enemy, so they drove three trucks into the creeks to create a makeshift bridge to cross the river one by one. Some slipped into the water, got soaked, and climbed back out. Those who could not pull themselves out of the water sank to the muddy bottom which became their grave.

A lack of cohesion within the military resulted in Japan's stunning defeat in the Battle of Wuyuan.

Meanwhile, around my father's Salaqi Station, Huang Youngchang of the Eighth Route Army entered Salaqi Castle and cut the electrical cables, breaking communication.

"Stationmaster, please come here!" My father was called and ran to find a soldier frozen in terror, unable to speak or move his eyes. Even his nerves had stopped functioning, and he was standing straight like a log. He could not move his body at all. Another Japanese soldier in ragged clothing emerged from a corner where he had been taking shelter and hung onto my father groaning but unable to speak. Inside the shelter were human limbs and blood in piles.

Dead bodies littered the shelter. Anger swelled in my father.

"How many soldiers died in the battle?"

"Stationmaster, it is not the time to count the dead."

"But the souls will not rest in peace this way. They fought and died pitifully, and still they are not counted among the dead."

"Stationmaster! We should attend to survivors. We must hurry. It looks like that man is frostbitten and cannot move."

"Okay. Carry him to the station right away."

They carried him from Salaqi Station to Baotou Station, and to the military hospital in Baotou.

The Battle of Wuyuan

At the military hospital, there were many soldiers who had been stabbed with bayonets and managed to survive. Many had frostbite all over their bodies, while many others had lost limbs or eyeballs and had become disabled for life.

Commander-in-Chief of Special Service Agency Kuwahara, his assistant Ichinosuke Shinohara, and about a dozen soldiers were cremated while over 50 Japanese policemen remained buried under the frozen soil. The Japanese military left the land of Wuyuan without picking up their remains, never to return.

This fact was forever etched into the memory of those who were involved in the Battle of Wuyuan.

General Fu Zuoyi is said to have been given the highest decoration from Chiang Kai-shek for his distinguished performance.

When my father returned from the Battle of Wuyuan, Lieutenant Miyagawa of the army infantry, the education staff officer for the Mongolian Garrison Army, had taken office. He was Prince Kitashirakawa.

The military police chief introduced my father to him explaining that my father performed very well working with the army as the stationmaster of Salaqi during the fighting at Wuyuan.

"I appreciate your hard work," the prince said with a gentle smile.

"And he teaches judo to our military policemen. He also performed a karate demonstration at the time of the foundation of Manchukuo," the military police chief added proudly, as if talking about himself.

"I would like to see the performance," the prince said, showing great interest. He added, "We are planning to hold an air defense seminar for the policemen. After that, I would like to see it." My father was delighted and respectfully agreed to perform.

Fire at the Railway Company House on Dong'an Street

Hinomoto Shrine

Military Policeman Miyamoto and his fiancé Naoko decided to hold a private wedding ceremony on March 3rd, the day of Japan's Doll Festival.

They married, of course, without informing the military police. Miyamoto might be killed any day; he desperately wanted an heir. Even if he could not obtain permission for his marriage from the military police, he felt he needed to leave proof of his existence in this world. His strong desire for a child moved Naoko.

However, even if it was a secret marriage, a wedding day was a special day, a 'once in a lifetime' event for a woman. My mother strongly wished for Naoko to wear a bridal kimono. Fortunately, she had her full wardrobe of wedding kimono sent from home. When she showed them to Naoko, the engaged younger woman was delighted.

On the day before the private wedding, the two ladies tried on the kimono for the last time in front of the tiered stand which displayed *hina* dolls. Carefully holding a handful of the kimono, Naoko said, "Thank you for helping me tomorrow. See you." She bowed low and left.

After Naoko had left, my mother put her two daughters to bed, cleaned up, and took a break at about half past ten. Suddenly, smoke rose from the bathroom and fire shot up. Without thinking, my mother held my sister and me under her arms and ran out the door. Immediately, the *hina* stand collapsed into the red hot flames.

We took shelter at a barber shop across the street.

"Fire! Fire!" Neighbors came out onto the street and soon a large crowd surrounded our house.

"Madam, are there any valuables inside?"

"My only important possessions are these girls."

The company house where we lived was located at No. 10 on Dong'an Street of Zhangjiakou. It was a bustling street with rows of buildings including the Zhangjiakou Military Police headquarters, Japanese Hotel Fujiya, an opera theater, Western and Japanese companies, a kimono shop, and a photo studio.

It could have attracted a huge crowd, but the military police, led by its chief, came promptly to deal with the incident, followed by other units stationed in Zhangjiakou.

A bucket relay from a well, 500 meters from Dong'an Street where the fire started, proved effective. A fire-fighting team, military officers,

Fire at the Railway Company House on Dong'an Street

neighbors, and 40 students of Koa Gakuin gathered together. Even rickshaw drivers left their rickshaws and pitched in. A large number of people working together in unison, shouting directions and encouragement, made a row of 500 meters to pass along water buckets to extinguish the flames.

The fire had briefly rose violently, fanned by a strong wind, and spread to two neighboring houses. It continued to burn for about three hours, finally getting extinguished at around half past one in the morning.

Luckily, the fire did not spread wider, and there were no casualties. Tremendous cooperation by many people helped minimize the effect.

My father was away at that time, involved in the Battle of Wuyuan.

My mother could not think of any reason why the fire might have occurred. According to the investigation, it was caused by the chimney of the stove which had gotten clogged and overheated.

In those days, many houses had an *ondol* system of wood heat that circulated underneath flooring. Many had poor chimney ventilation, blocking the flow of smoke which in turn led to smoldering wood that could poison people from the smoke or cause a fire by overheating the chimney.

The *ondol* stove was very different from the *pechka* we had in Harbin.

When my mother visited the Consulate General Police to explain the fire, Miyamoto accompanied her. The interview at the police was very brief, and they showed sympathy for her saying that they were glad that she had not been injured.

The private wedding of Miyamoto and Naoko was held as planned at Hinomoto Shrine. Naoko, in my mother's bridal kimono that had escaped the flames, was glowing. My mother accompanied her in the most ordinary clothes she could find.

Airplane Crash at Qinghe River

Monument dedicated to Prince Kitashirakawa

The family celebrated the first birthday of the second daughter, me, in good health, but by summer's end I had fallen ill and lost weight day by day.

As the hospital in Zhangjiakou couldn't make a diagnosis, I was sent to a hospital in Beijing, and hospitalized immediately. Even under treatment in a hospital bed, I my condition worsened. I lied outstretched on my bed like a dried-up frog. My face was pale. When my arm or thigh muscles were pinched or pulled, they stretched out like the infirm skin of an elderly woman.

My cry, once so loud that it could have vibrated the window glass of my hospital room, was weakening.

Diet therapy was the only treatment for me, but my bowel movements became more and more irregular.

Getting nutrition via an IV, my thin baby arms became stiff with marks left from injection needles. Even so, the nutrient injections were not enough. To provide nutrition and give me energy, my mother tried to feed me some mashed potatoes or mashed apples, but they just moved through my system undigested.

I was suffering from infant malnutrition. Many children, especially bottle-fed children, contracted nutritional disorders due to various stomach allergies.

But I had been breast-fed, so if there were any reason for the nutritional disorder, it eluded the medical staff. The doctor said he was not sure why I was suffering from malnutrition. The problem just might be extreme sensitivity.

Naoko visited my mother at the hospital in Beijing. It seemed God might have answered the prayer of Military Policeman Miyamoto; Naoko had become pregnant.

However, since the marriage was a secret to the military police, she avoided giving birth in Zhangjiakou where the police were stationed. Instead, she stayed with an acquaintance in Beijing. The host father who was working at Kahoku Traffic Headquarters in Beijing was living with his wife. The couple had no children. They warmly welcomed Naoko like their own daughter.

Naoko often came to see my mother at my hospital, play with my sister, and give some advice for the baby from a nurse's point of view.

Something the doctor in Beijing did not understand was that we did not have a water supply system in Zhangjiakou when I was born. Water vendors were selling water in large wooden barrels on the right and left sides of their single-wheeled vehicles, peacefully whistling along with the creaking of the wheel.

The autumn sky of Beijing shone clear blue. The air was pleasantly dry. The stars twinkling across the night sky looked as if they could be reached by one's fingertips and plucked out of the sky.

Under such a beautiful sky, it was unbearable for my mother to see her beloved daughter declining without any way to help.

My father suggested that she come home before the cold season. My mother nervously suggested that to her doctor. He seemed to have already given up hope, and said, "It may be better for her to spend time at home and be taken care of there." He didn't even try to discourage her.

"The doctor told me to be spend time with the baby, but how long is she expected to live? If she is not destined to recover, I will see her off to heaven at home with her father," she thought sadly. Thus, it was decided to return home in Zhangjiakou with me as the baby who might die any day.

On the day before I was discharged, my mother bought a roll of cloth for a new dress. It was a pale pink base printed with countless cranes in red and white.

My mother thought about dressing me in a kimono at my funeral, but instead she bought material covered with cranes, the symbol of longevity to Japanese. She held out hope for the miracle of a long life for me.

When I was discharged from the hospital, Naoko came to see us off at Beijing Station.

While at home, the water was discovered to be the cause of the illness. Similar symptoms were discovered in other sensitive babies. And just like that the symptoms that had me bedridden and caused my family to almost lose hope disappeared after the water was properly purified.

My mother was expecting another baby two months later in November, and Naoko was having her baby in February the following year. Naoko was reluctant to leave. My mother suggested that they later present each other with a healthy baby and promised that she would make a kimono for Naoko's baby for *miya mairi*, the ceremonial first visit to a shrine. They exchanged goodbyes, wishing each other good health.

They had thought they would get together again during the season of the Doll Festival after the New Year. That was their intention. But, as fate would have it, the two women never saw each other again.

My mother got on a train to Zhangjiakou.

When she crossed the Great Wall for the first time, the baby had not been born yet. "When I travel this way again someday in the future, my baby might no longer exist," she thought with great sadness while gazing at the passing scenery out her window.

Her frail eldest daughter was sitting beside her.

A vendor at Nankou Station had a basket stacked with large persimmons. Their orange-ish color struck her as particularly vivid.

Xuanhua grapes and Nankou persimmons were famous for their quality. Xuanhua grapes were large with a clear light green color. Nankou persimmons were shiny and large. They were sweet in their natural state, but also delicious frozen. Families would take advantage of the frigid climate by placing fully ripened ones outside the window and later eat them by scooping the cold, sweet orange slush with a spoon, like eating a sherbet.

When my mother came to Zhangjiakou over the Great Wall for the first time, my father was standing in the middle of the station platform with a basketful of Nankou persimmons. For a rustic man, this was the quintessential way to welcome a woman.

It was persimmon season again. This time my mother leaned out of the train window and bought a bagful of Nankou persimmons for my father.

On September 4th, the day after his wife and young daughters had come back from Beijing, my father took his eldest daughter for a walk on the bank of the Qingshui River. The sky was perfectly cloudless.

Walking with her father hand in hand for the first time in several months, my sister was all smiles. Her cool, round eyes darted to look here and there and she sometimes skipped down the road.

The Qingshui River was a grand river several hundred meters wide running vertically through the center of Zhangjiakou. One could hardly catch a glimpse of the actual river water, however, as reddish soil and

Airplane Crash at Qinghe River

grass fields covered the area.

Military drills often took place along this river. The river's east side was lined with government buildings and city offices of Mengjiang United Autonomous Government and the Northern China Development company. Some Japanese high officials, including Masayoshi Ohira who would later become prime minister, had been sent from Japan to work in one of these governmental offices.

Close to them was Daping Park with a greenhouse and flower beds which always displayed pretty flowers. The cosmos were blooming spectacularly, as if competing for a grand prize.

On that day, military training was being held on the upper river bank of Qinghe-dahanxiang Bridge. This reminded father of the time when he met Prince Kitashirakawa after the educational training for aircraft spotters and his promise to put on a martial arts performance for the prince.

He sat down near the bridge with his daughter to watch the training for awhile.

In the middle of the riverbed in the distance, about 100 aircraft spotters comprised of the military officers of each unit and policemen had lined up. Commanding at the center in front of them was Prince Kitashirakawa, accompanied by Lieutenant Colonel Tsukiyama, and a military attaché standing one step behind the prince. A military policeman was on guard.

The training on that day was air-to-ground and air-to-air training. Reconnaissance planes had been brought in for the training. The lecture on air-to-ground attacks and instruction had not been finished when, suddenly, one of the planes made a sudden turn. Its nose lowered and, flying near ground level, headed straight toward the prince.

No! Without thinking my father grabbed his daughter who had been sitting by his side and held her tight.

No! In an instant, a military policeman leapt at the prince from behind to knock him to the ground, but the plane was an instant faster. Prince Kitashirakawa and Lieutenant Colonel Tsukiyama had their legs swept up in the air, and they fell violently onto the ground. Some of the nearby military officers were also struck.

The plane continued to head into the line of aircraft spotters from the front, mowing down many officers before crashing with a loud explosion.

The wings were bent, the body of the plane was shattered to pieces, and the engine was thrown from the plane.

The loud explosion prompted people to rush out of the buildings along the river.

The crash site turned into an inferno.

Amid great shock and confusion, the prince, the military attaché, and other casualties were taken to the military hospital.

Later that night, Kempei Miyamoto came to see my father.

Prince Kitashirakawa was seriously injured and lost a considerable amount of blood. Despite the best effort of the military hospital staff, he passed away in the evening of the same day. Military Attaché Tsukiyama was also severely injured, but he survived.

Five or six officers died. Including light injuries, there were more than ten casualties.

The headquarters of the Mongolia Garrison Army fell into turmoil.

General Commander Nishio, General Chief of Staff of the China Expeditionary Army Itagaki, Area Army Commander Tada, and other officers flew into Zhangjiakou one after another, filling up the airport.

News of the unexpected plane crash hit the headquarters of the Mongolian Garrison Army and the whole town of Zhangjiakou with bewilderment and sadness.

It was decided to send the body of Prince Kitashirakawa to Tokyo.

On the next day, a funeral was held at the Army Headquarters in Zhangjiakou, and on the morning of the following day, a special hearse plane flew out of town before disappearing into the eastern sky. A large crowd gathered to see the plane off.

A special train was parked at Zhangjiakou Station.

"Hisataka-kun, come here." My father was called by the stationmaster and boarded the train where he found a seat slightly larger than one tatami mat at the center. It was solemnly built, looking like a high-quality bed.

"What is this?" my father asked.

"Can you lie down on it?" My father did as told, lying on the bed on his back, and stretched his arms and legs comfortably. The stationmaster was looking at him for a while with his arms crossed, and murmured, "Ah, it must be a space to place a coffin on."

On hearing "a space to place a coffin on," my father jumped up. The stationmaster explained.

Late at night of the same day of the plane accident, the Mongolia Garrison Army Headquarters requested that he urgently arrange a special train to Beijing. He was told that it should be strictly kept a secret.

He was not allowed to ask any questions, including for what purpose or with what contents. The fact that the headquarters made the request should also be kept secret. Should anyone else learn about this train, they could not guarantee the safety of the stationmaster. The order sounded threatening.

At that point, the stationmaster still did not know of the passing of Prince Kitashirakawa.

He was ordered to run a special train, but it was not so easy. He first had to reschedule various matters, including the scheduling of other trains. However, considering the urgent secret request by Army Headquarters, he understood that his duty was to execute a grave task. Immediately, he reported that to the director and gathered the managers responsible for general administration, transportation, and railcars. They spent the entire night arranging a special train in secret, and were fully ready for the order to run the train at any time.

They were waiting for the order all day, but did not hear anything from Army Headquarters. As the plan was secret, they could make no inquiry.

Meanwhile, the death of Prince Kitashirakawa became public. Amid the confusion and turmoil, Army Headquarters deliberated carefully on how to carry the prince's body back to Japan. The suggestion was made that the body be sent to Beijing by train, and then fly off to Japan from Beijing in a large airplane.

It was found out later that the coffin had been downsized to fit the small plane that was to fly from Zhangjiakou. Thus, the special hearse plane left Zhangjiakou that morning flying directly to Japan.

On the train that had been prepped to be used as a hearse, the stationmaster and my father talked about their sorrow for Prince Kitashirakawa and the plane accident.

It had become a morning custom for Prince Kitashirakawa to leave his temporary residence and go to Army Headquarters on horseback. On his way to his office, the stationmaster greeted the prince at the station's railroad crossing. The stationmaster was looking out for the safety of the prince as he crossed. The prince always responded to the greeting politely.

The stationmaster would no longer have the chance to respectfully greet him in the morning or see his familiar smile.

Moreover, my father forever lost his chance to perform his martial art demonstration to the prince.

The two men shed tears of grief.

"But the prince has a boy who will succeed his father," the stationmaster said, as if consoling himself. That strengthened my father's wish to have an heir. "This time, I will definitely have a boy," he prayed.

People in Zhangjiakou talked about the prince who had been seen taking relaxed walks around town in the evening twilight, or on residential streets in private clothes, accompanied by a single attendant.

A monument for Prince Kitashirakawa was erected on the riverbed where the plane accident had occurred. When passing by the monument at the center of the bridge, people stopped to bow deeply and show respect.

Mengjiang Shrine was founded to enshrine the soul of Prince Kitashirakawa. The military attaché was elevated to priest to console and protect the prince's soul. A memorial hall was also established.

One life in vibrant health perished in one instant, and a weak life on the verge of death unexpectedly held on for a long time.

The red fruit of persimmons may have become my blood. Persimmons were said to cool a body and be difficult to digest. My mother often avoided giving them to me. But I refused any food other than the red ripened Nankou persimmons which I sucked happily, and regained my energy little by little.

After the plane accident, on September 15th, the new water supply system was completed. And with it, the digestive disorder inflicting especially sensitive babies and causing malnutrition, disappeared.

Zhangjiakou was to develop into the leading city for politics and finance in the Mengjiang region.

Birth of the Son

In November, the cold weather of Zhangjiakou grew even severer.

Due to its continental climate, spring and fall in Zhangjiakou were short, and summer was cool. People called the city "Karuizawa—a popular summer resort in Japan—of Mengjiang in Northern China."

 However, the winter season was long and bitterly cold. Thin ice was already forming on the surface of the Qinghe River.

Meanwhile, a new life was about to be born.

On the night of his third child's birth, my father was at home—a very rare occurrence.

He was out of town on business when his first daughter was born in Harbin. When his second daughter was born here in Zhangjiakou, he was again not at home, busily dealing with duties due to the battles around Khalkhin Gol.

On the evening of the latest birth, he was preparing to go home after rigorous training at the Kahoku Traffic Judo Club.

Club members started to talk about the baby about to be delivered.

"So, it will be third time lucky," one of them said, sympathizing with my father's strong wish to have a boy.

"No, what happens twice will happen three times," another member said, offering a truly unwelcome opinion.

While feeling strongly he would be granted a boy this time, he sometimes felt a slight sense of unease that the baby might, after all, again be a girl. He was struggling with such doubts when he was heard, "What happens twice will happen three times." The quip upset him. The man who said that had two boys in a row and was gloating. Just having sons made my father resent him.

"Huh? What did you say? Say that again!" my father said as if fully ready to fight.

"Hey, calm down," the man replied. Then the man who had said "third time lucky" stepped in to separate the two.

"Grappling should take place in the dojo, but practice is over for today," he said. And to the man who had said "What happens twice will happen three times," he said, "Some things should remain unsaid."

"I just thought it would save him from disappointment if his wish is denied," the man said, which was even more wicked to my father.

Birth of the Son

That night, the baby was born.

"Third time lucky" called it correctly.

My father doze off.

Dreaming, he saw a vast blue ocean spread into infinity. Then, from far over the horizon, a large treasure boat was heading toward him. It was coming closer and closer, and, with a huge rolling wave, the treasure boat came into the house from the entrance. The splash of the wave rushed toward him.

"There, a boy."

The midwife herself announced the birth of a new life in a husky male voice, which awakened my father. He rushed into the next room.

"YES! A boy! It's a boy! It's a boy!" Then he kept close to the midwife bathing the baby in the tub, saying, "Hey, gently, gently, yes, that's good..."

"Oh, no, no, don't treat him roughly. His balls may fall off and turn him into a girl!"

The midwife, who had 30 years' experience helping childbirth countless times in both Japan and abroad, almost dropped the baby in the bathwater.

"Infants are not paper dolls. His balls cannot drop off and he can't transform into a girl just like that!"

The midwife came to my mother's bed in a fit of laughter. My mother felt tension dissipating from her body. She thought, "Now I have fulfilled my role." She felt she could get up and move immediately.

My father was in high spirits.

On his way to work the next morning, he stopped everyone he saw and proudly talked about the birth of his son.

"Now I've got a baby boy."

"Good morning, good morning. My son was born last night."

To a Chinese man who was absentmindedly pushing a unicycle, my father cheerfully said "Good morning!" raising his hand in greeting. This startled the old dirty-faced laborer who timidly smiled back at my father.

When he reached the train station where he worked, he shared his happiness even more openly. To not only his co-workers but all the staff working in the station building, and even the passengers passing through Zhangjiakou Station, he kept excitedly talking about his newly born son.

"I've got a baby boy. You know what, my wife is a great woman. She made me worried for the first and second times, but this third time, she has given me a beautiful baby boy."

It was our family tradition that, in the first days of every new year, we had a New Year's family picture taken in formal clothing at the photo studio in front of the railway office. In the family picture of that year, one and a half months after the birth, my father is holding an infant in a pure white blanket as if it were a treasure.

He took the baby everywhere, even when the baby was still in diapers. Once when the baby peed on a geisha's lap at a party, he happily said his son would become a great man in the future.

Later, my mother visited the young geisha to apologize and handed her some money to cover the laundry fee for her kimono. With the birth of my brother, a bright ray of light shone into our home. Our daily lives centered around caring for the newborn boy.

Miyamoto, who had come to see the baby boy after hearing the news, shared the joy repeatedly with my father by drinking toast after toast. He did not, however, visit us during the New Year holiday. He used to say that he and my father would drink a toast when Miyamoto had a boy, and my father had been looking forward to that as well. He was wondering what Miyamoto was doing when, after one week in January, Military Policeman Yasuda came to visit my father. He was also one of his judo students who had obtained a dan rank.

Yasuda said Miyamoto had been missing since the end of the last year.

He had thought that there was no need to worry, and that Miyamoto would come back triumphantly with a great achievement, but it seemed Miyamoto had gone too deeply into enemy territory.

At that time, they had information that the Eighth Route Army of the Chinese Communist Party seemed to have formed a secret organization to destroy the Mengjiang Government, and had started its rebellion. Miyamoto had been spying on them when he disappeared.

The kempei-tai did everything they could, but they could not locate him.

They even sent a Chinese prisoner into enemy territory. According to the information clandestinely obtained, Miyamoto had gone into enemy territory and was spying throughout the night. It was extremely cold with

Birth of the Son

an especially severe northern wind. Battling the cold, his inability to stifle a cough betrayed him. The enemy pounced. They had been suspicious about spies. A cough—what a mortifying failure it was! But that weather really could freeze people to their bones.

The enemy seemed to have been enticing Miyamoto from the beginning. He was a thorn in their side. This information seemed true. Even as *Setsubun*—a holiday celebrated at the traditional start of spring in Japan on February 3rd—was approaching, they waited. Naoko's expected childbirth was soon, but still Miyamoto did not come home.

For all they knew, he had already been shot to death, beheaded, or was being tortured in confinement.

Naoko successfully gave birth to a boy on *Setsubun*. It was the boy Miyamoto had been long-awaiting. My father went to Beijing, and told Naoko about Miyamoto.

She did not shed tears. She listened to my father silently, and bravely said that Miyamoto had wanted to have a boy to be his heir out of anxiety.

My father named the boy "Kenichiro" because Miyamoto had been the best (*ichi*) man in the military police (*kempeitai*).

Naoko said she would go home to Nagasaki and raise the baby to be a good man, fulfilling Miyamoto's ambition.

My father went to the military police and made them compensate Naoko and her baby to cover their living expenses for some time.

My mother wanted to say goodbye to Naoko, but could not go to Beijing with her three young children. Wishing happiness for Naoko and her baby, my mother sewed a ceremonial kimono for his *miya mairi*, ceremonial first visit to a shrine, as she had promised, and asked my father to bring it to Naoko.

It was a black kimono marked with the family crests, with a pattern of a ferocious eagle spreading its wings wide. On the lining were Mt. Fuji and the rising sun.

Whenever my mother thought of Naoko, she felt sad.

After some time, my mother received a letter from Naoko.

It said that Kenichiro was growing healthily. She was warmly supported by people around her, and she was working as a nurse. She was spending calm days of prayer, gazing every day at Urakami Cathedral in the distance, praying for Miyamoto's soul to rest in peace.

On December 8th of that year, Pearl Harbor was attacked and the Great East Asian War—the Pacific theater of World War II—began.

The Imperial Army talked up its glorious successes every day.

When I was born, my two-year older sister said, "Oh, such a sweet baby," and soon became a caring sister, making our mother happy and relieved. In my case, however, I was different when my brother was born one year after my birth.

While I was in hospital in Beijing, my mother was always cradling me in bed as I slept. Even after I was discharged from hospital, I had not yet fully recovered. And I still wanted to sleep with my mother.

Each time my mother fed my baby brother, I snuggled up onto her lap. Each time, my mother gave one breast to the baby, and another to me saying, "OK, this breast is yours," or "This breast is for the baby, and this is for you."

Speaking soothingly, my mother held her two youngest in both arms and offered her breasts.

As I always imitated her saying "This is your breast" or "One breast for you," I came to call myself "you."

In those days we called our father *"totto"* and our mother *"kakka."* Visitors would laugh saying, "What a family! Being called *totto* and *kakka* like a family of crows living in a hen house!"

But my mother nonchalantly replied, "Isn't it adorable? It's only for a short period that they will cutely call us that."

As mother predicted, *"totto"* developed to *"tottan,"* *"kakka"* to *"kattan,"* and later were improved into *"tochan"* and *"kachan."* And finally we started to properly say *"otoochan* (Daddy)" and *"okaachan* (Mommy)."

However, as for myself, I kept calling myself 'you' until I entered elementary school.

With an abundance of affection from both parents, the newborn baby grew up to be a healthy and happy boy.

My father's love for the boy was great. He would hold the still crawling baby on his lap, lay him flat, grab his ankles while bending and

Birth of the Son

stretching his legs, or give his body a loving rubdown. Once the baby started to toddle, my father let him fall on the tatami and stand back up, as a father tiger would play with his cub. In the end, despite the fact the boy was just starting to walk, my father could not wait any longer and started to teach his son the basics of karate.

In addition, my father took the boy many places.

When a camel caravan came to the riverbank outside Dajingmen Gate ringing their bells, he promptly took the boy outside to see the travelers in high spirits.

When a camel stood up, it appeared much taller and bigger than expected, dwarfing the view provided when it was sitting flat on the ground peacefully after several big bags had been taken off.

My father was tall, but still needed to stand tippy-toed to hold his son in place on the back of the camel. It stood still with its head high, looking ahead with round black eyes.

In contrast, a Mongolian horse was short and easy for my father to sit the boy on its back. If my father sat on its back, his feet could reach the ground. Despite their diminutive size, these Mongolian horses fiercely compete with each other at Naadam, a largest festival in Mongolia, and gallop strongly around the Mongolian plains.

An idea hit my father that he should show his son Mongolian horses in full stride, and one day he took the boy to a horse race track. It was his first time to visit such a place. Confused about what to do in front of the ticket counter, a neatly dressed young man asked him if he could help.

My father said, "Oh, thank you. Please take this and buy some tickets," and handed money from his wallet to the man.

However, the man never returned.

My father held the boy and waited and waited to no avail. His money was lost to the young thief.

When he was again in need, this time a more serious bind, another man came up to him, accompanied by two or three others.

The man's name was Bao Taibao.

"What would you say if I asked you to give me the boy?" he said in a very high-handed manner.

"Whaaat!" Asked if he would give up his son, my father was outraged like a fire burning out of control.

Then Bao Taibao stared for a while at my father who was holding his son tightly and then said, in a peaceful tone this time, "Kidnapping is a common means for ransom. If you love your son, you should be careful. You can be targeted any time."

As Bao Taibao was leaving, my father called and stopped him.

"Wait a minute. From today, I ask you to guard my son. Please. If anything happens to him, take full responsibility."

Bao Taibao was taken aback with a vacant look, and then laughed out loud.

"You are a funny man. I am the head of the mounted bandits."

"Yes, that is the very reason I am asking you. There's no place as safe as with you."

Bao Taibao stared at my father and the boy again, and then grinned.

"I will arrange your ride home."

One of his followers immediately arranged a *yangche* rickshaw for my father to return home with body guards in the front, back, right, and left of the vehicle.

It was my father's first encounter with Bao Taibao, man to man.

Yungang Grottoes

Yungang Grottoes

In 1942, my father had been promoted to head assistant stationmaster for Datong Station.

The city of Datong, noted for Yungang Grottoes, had been the capital during the Northern Wei era and a military stronghold since ancient times. It was surrounded by a well-fortified castle on a plateau 1,000 meters above sea level.

A Buddhist temple is curved into the Wuzhou mountain cliffs. In those days, a team of researchers from Kyoto University was studying the Yungang Grottoes.

When Hideki Tojo entered the Datong Castle, he commanded to never touch the stone Buddhist statues in the name of the commander-in-chief of the Japanese Imperial Army.

At the time of the Marco Polo Bridge Incident, the Japanese Army occupied Datong, and the Kahoku Traffic Company was assigned to govern transportation in the area. They were providing cooperation and logistical support. They also distributed train tickets, food, and daily supplies to the research team at Datong Station.

On the other hand, although Datong was known as a Buddhist city due to its stone Buddha statues, it was also an industrial city rich with underground resources from its coal mine. For developing and constructing the Datong Coal Mine, there had been an influx of Japanese workers, including highly skilled engineers working for Japanese companies such as Datong Thermal Power Plant and Mengjiang Cement Industries.

At Datong Station, there was always an array of freight trains with good quality coals piled up.

Word of the setbacks of the Japanese Army in recent battles trickled in, but compared to Salaqi district, public order of Datong was still stable.

The 26th Division Army based in Manchuria was stationed in Datong.

Like the time in Zhangjiakou, the army soldiers and military policemen came to my father by turns, and absorbed themselves in practicing judo. In those days, judo and kendo were actively practiced at every railroad office. Inter-office matches between different stations were held.

A dojo was built at the Datong Police Station, and its workers were practicing judo and kendo there.

Yungang Grottoes

My father opened not just the station's dojo but also the living quarters to practitioners. Soldiers and military policemen were always visiting him at home, holding and playing with his son or singing folk songs with his eldest daughter who was now in kindergarten.

Those visits provided a temporary respite for the soldiers.

In those days, groups of Japanese with an interest in Chinese culture such as scholars and painters occasionally visited Datong to see the Yungang Grottoes. My father decided to show this world heritage site to his eldest daughter.

He was given permission to share a ride on a military truck to the grottoes. The soldiers on the truck were excited to ride with a cute girl and warmly welcomed her. Throughout the 17 kilometer drive to the stone Buddha statutes, the truck rumbled down the road with all the passengers singing children's songs together.

One of the soldiers was pretty much shouting rather than singing. He was shedding tears gustily and sentimentally singing out *Ame Furi Otsuki-san* (Mr. Moon in the Rain) toward the high-noon sun.

One day, a man who stole a ride on the train was captured at Datong Station. He was in poor Chinese laborer clothes. His piercing gaze straight into my father's eyes gave him the impression that he had seen him before.

He then remembered an incident.

When the freight train robbery occurred at Supingkai Station in Mantetsu, one of the captured shouted, "We will take back this country someday!" It was the look of the leader of an anti-Manchurian and anti-Japanese guerrilla group.

The eyes of the captured resembled those of that leader, hiding rage inside.

Immediately my father said, "Hey, I haven't seen you for a while. Thank you for coming."

To the station staff who had brought the captured, he said, "This is my good friend."

In the station staff room, my father said to the Chinese man, "I have to go deal with an urgent matter. I'm sorry but please eat this and wait for me."

He handed over a lunchbox and left the room.

After a while, he returned to the room to find that the man had gone. The lunchbox was completely empty.

"Assistant Stationmaster, was it all right that we released him?" the station staff said.

It was clear that the Chinese man was not my father's good friend. Having wasted his effort in capturing a freeloader, the station staff was not happy.

"Besides, he did not look like an ordinary citizen…"

"You are observant. You noticed that he was someone special."

"I'm worried about the consequences. Won't he seek revenge?"

"It'll be fine. Releasing a small man would cause troubles later—but a big man will be fine. A big man has a big man's pride," my father explained.

Then he continued saying, "However, I am sorry for wasting your exploit. I will treat you to dinner tonight to make up for it, so please forgive me. I have skipped lunch today."

A second son was born on August 8th, 1943.

My mother had already fulfilled her role as a dutiful wife by giving birth to the first son. She was feeling lighter, not having to worry about whether the baby was a boy or a girl. However, the birth of the second boy made my father, who had again strongly wished for a boy, overjoyed.

Saying that the brothers could practice martial arts together, and that they would make partners in pair-form competitions, he was looking at the newly born baby as if he wanted to get the baby up and working out immediately.

As my father was an only child, it brought extreme joy knowing that his first son now had a brother. Besides, the baby's birthday was the 8th day of the 8th month (August) in the 8th year of Showa (1943), having three eights. Eight, in kanji, is written "八", a shape that broadens toward the bottom. Japanese believed this represented increasing success. "What a blessed boy! This boy will make a name for himself when he grows up."

One night my mother came home with the baby boy bundled with so many hopes in her arms.

They were promptly brought back down to earth when their elder son became violently ill. He threw up thick white liquid and was writhing in agony.

My shocked father immediately took him to Datong Hospital.

"Oh, I see. This is serious. Yes, it's cholera. No doubt, that's it," Doctor Oyabe diagnosed with certainty.

"*Taitai* (Madam)! Here, I found this." A babysitter, a young Chinese girl, brought a toy box to my mother who looked inside the box.

"What are these?"

"Castor beans."

"Castor beans?" On the girl's palm, my mother saw four or five oval beans that looked like pinto beans.

"I think the boy ate them."

In those days, Northern China had the slogan, "Increase public safety by growing castor beans." Growing those beans was vigorously encouraged.

Castor beans are the ingredients of castor oil, a thick, bitter and powerful laxative all children endured at one time or another. The oil from the castor-oil plant was used in aircraft fuels.

They grew very easily. By just burying them in the soil anywhere, on house gardens or vacant lots, without fertilizer, they bore large beautiful leaves, and their seeds made oil.

While the Second Sino-Japanese War was dragging out, Japan faced the need to win the "Great East Asia War"—World War II—as well. They needed fuel for aircrafts. To that end, citizens were encouraged to grow at least one or two castor-oil-plants on whatever small space they could find—in yards or office gardens, schoolyards, or even around train stations. The goal was to provide the raw materials for aircraft fuels to support the war that would beat the brutal American and British armies.

Castor beans looked similar to pinto beans and were often mistaken for them. My mother had heard about a young woman who had moved to this region when her husband transferred here. She tried to boil beans, but they never became soft and could not be eaten. There was also a story of a small child who had eaten them by mistake and very nearly died.

My mother was in a panic.

"What did you do with these? Did he eat them?" My mother asked me in an unusually demanding manner, which almost made me cry.

Earlier that afternoon, an older girl in our neighborhood invited my brother and I to her playhouse. She was an active, cute girl. She said, "Now you are my guests. Please eat these," and placed toy plates with beans on them before us.

With her urging us on, I put one of the beans into my mouth. It was so bitter that I immediately spat it out.

"What about your brother? Did he eat them? Did he?!" My mother looked into my eyes, demanding to know.

"He ate them. He is a boy, so he was patient and ate them," I said. Yes, a boy should never whine about food being good or bad. That's what our father was always teaching him. As a result, my brother ate the beans without even complaining about their bitterness.

On hearing "He ate them," my mother snatched the castor beans from the palm of the Chinese girl and dashed outside.

The railway company housing was inside the castle walls, and Datong Hospital and Datong Station were outside. When my mother went out, the station servant boy Wang always fetched a *yangche* rickshaw or had a car arranged at Datong Station.

"No time to spare. I cannot wait. Running should be faster," she decided immediately, and ran at full speed back on the same road where she had proudly come holding her second son just a few hours before. It had been less than one week since childbirth. Holding her belly, and still feeling tired from giving birth, she stopped several times to recover her breathe, and started running again furiously. The edge of her kimono loosened.

When she rushed into the hospital panting, she heard my father's excited voice.

"This is my son. Why do you try to take him away from me?"

"Cholera is infectious. A patient with an infectious illness must be isolated."

"Then isolate me with him," he demanded. To be sure, cholera is an infectious disease that demands isolation of the patient. Indeed, my brother's symptoms were very similar to cholera: violent vomiting of a cloudy white liquid along with fever and diarrhea. Any doctor would have diagnosed cholera.

The castor beans my mother brought solved the crisis. They could return home with their precious son. On the wide and dark road of Datong, the ancient capital, two *yangche* rickshaws ran at full speed back toward the walled castle. In the front *yangche* was my father tightly holding his son, and on the following *yangche* was my exhausted mother, her body deeply slouching in the seat. She could hear the rhythmical footsteps of the rickshaw pullers as if they were running in the distance.

Doctor Oyabe asked a retired nurse, who was living in the same railroad living quarters as my father, to attend to my brother for that night.

Despite the midnight hour, the ex-nurse gladly attended to the boy all night long. After his vomiting and diarrhea stopped, he wanted to drink water. He sat up and drank, and then slept again for some time, and then sat up again to drink water, repeating this process. In due course his condition improved.

Immediately, Bao Taibao arrived.

It was a matter of grave significance for his young lord. He came accompanied by three followers, with a large basket full of eggs and a sheep roasted whole.

"You have two boys. That's unfair. Could I have one? I will raise him to be a great man."

Since this day, every time Bao Taibao visited us or saw my father, he kept asking my father to give him one of the boys, saying he would raise him to be a great man.

Maidazhao and Hohhot

Zhenjue Temple, constructed in the Qing Dynasty (Hohhot)

When my father became the stationmaster of Maidazhao, our family moved to Hohhot, avoiding the instability and lack of public safety in his work area. Hohhot means *blue city* in Mongolian; blue is associated with the sky, eternity and purity in Mongolia.

Its Japanese name was *Kowagotoku*, which the Japanese abbreviated to "Kowa."

It was a beautiful city surrounded by such greenery that people could not imagine it a gateway to dessert. The city was divided into two parts; Guihuacheng was the old fortified city, and Suiyuancheng was the new upscale area. On both sides of the street between the two were riverside willows and old elm trees providing the town with a verdant cityscape.

Fluffy poplar flowers blown by the wind floated all over the sky like snowflakes.

The city hosted the famous Lamaism temples as well: Five Pagoda Temple and Da Zhao Temple. The grave of Wang Zhaojun, one of the "Four Beauties" of ancient China, was also in this region.

In April 1944, my sister entered elementary school.

My father found an excellent *landoseru,* a special backpack for schoolbooks.

It was a very pretty red bag displayed in the center of a Japanese bag shop in Hohhot.

"Wow," he murmured as soon as he laid eyes on it and quickly attempted to purchase it.

However, the shopkeeper flatly said, "This is not for sale."

My father insisted, "What? You have displayed it in your shop and you say you won't sell it. Anyway, I like it a lot. Please sell it to me for my daughter. You can charge me double, triple. Name your price."

However, the shopkeeper steadfastly refused, explaining that he could not sell it because it was for his daughter. He had, he said, made it for his daughter to celebrate her birth. It was such an excellent work that he wanted to show it off in his own shop without slightest intention of selling it.

Hearing this my father became even more obsessed with it saying that it was blessed with the shopkeeper's love and begged him to sell it to him.

Like a rock, the owner refused, explaining that, in some sense, it already belonged to his daughter.

The two strong-willed fathers went back and forth.

"For my daughter."

"No, for my daughter."

"My daughter is…"

"But my daughter is…"

As the two fathers bickered about the *landoseru*, and praised their respective daughters more lavishly, they found they had much in common.

After all, the *landoseru* fell into my father's hands. The shopkeeper's daughter was still a baby. My father praised the shopkeeper to the heavens encouraging the man to make an even better one with such splendid skill. While giving in to my father's appreciation for his work, he resolved to make further effort to produce an even better one for his own daughter.

In short, my father won by persistence.

With the red *landoseru* on her back, my sister Akiko entered a Japanese national elementary school in Hohhot. She was a cheerful and active girl as the two Chinese characters for Akiko—"bright + child"—suggested. She soon became a notable presence in her class. She had the top grades, and always performed the leading role in the athletic meets and school plays.

She always came home from school with her friends, among them children of Mongolian senior officers for the Mengjiang government, as well as Chinese children from our neighborhood.

When her friends were curious to see her Japanese toys like *otedama* bean bags, *chiyogami* paper, or *ohajiki* marbles, my sister who was full of a philanthropic spirit, generously encouraged them to take whatever they wanted. I would not have minded if she had only given away hers, but when all she had was gone, she told me to offer mine, distributing my toys to her friends.

I would not have cared to give one or two *ohajiki* marbles or *chiyogami* paper, but I did not want anyone else to touch my favorite *otedama* bean bags and the pretty flower patterned dolls my mother had made with pieces of cloth leftover from her sewing projects. When my sister came home with her friends, I would hastily gather all the toys I had been playing with and dash to the back room with them.

The first thing my sister did every morning was to go into the henhouse in our back yard, and put the freshly laid eggs into a basket, counting one, two, three, four, five, six. We took them to the station canteen that morning. By the time we came home from school, the eggs would have been transformed into a soft sponge cake and delivered to our home. Our 3 o'clock snack was always sponge cake.

Another of my favorite sweets was thick malt syrup. Its amber color filled up a jar. I would dip a spoon in, spin it around to whip up a thick thread of syrup, and suck it. Words cannot express how delicious it was.

On one broadcast anniversary day, my sister was invited to a radio station in Hohhot to read a story on the radio.

Her story was entitled "Saluting the Battleship." It was a story of a soldier on a battleship that had been bombed. With the glowing sun setting in the background, he raised a Japanese flag and clung to it as the ship and loyal soldier sank together into the sea. To prepare for her moment on the air, my sister practiced reading with her teacher every day after school. At home she also practiced hard by our mother's side.

On the day of the broadcast, my mother was listening intently to her daughter's voice on the radio, nodding to every phrase and sentence.

After the reading was finished, she was pleased, calling it splendid. She stood up happily and told me to join her to go pick up my sister.

When my sister finished reading and looked up, she took in the vivid sunset scene. It reminded her of the image of the Japanese flag fluttering on a black battleship that was slowly sinking into the sea.

In those days, the Northwest Research Institute, an educational institution to study inner Asia, had been established in Zhangjiakou. Its director was Kinji Imanishi of Kyoto University, and the staff included Tadao Umesao.

In Datong, researching Yungang Grottoes had been handed over to the 26th Division of the Imperial Army and was still ongoing.

Zhangjiakou, Datong, and our town of Hohhot were peaceful with stores stocked with plenty of materials and food. It was hard to imagine that it was in the middle of a war.

However, the Mongolian Army had been continuously fighting against the army led by Fu Zuoyi. In addition, the Eighth Route Army under the Chinese Communist Party and the Northeastern Advance Force led by the bandit Ma Zhanshan were secretly fighting for leadership in the war against Japan.

My father had been assigned to be the stationmaster of Maidazhao in Salaqi of Suiyuan Province, on the railway between Beiping and Baotou, and the chief of the "Airo" area in Maidazhao.

The goal in Airo was to pacify villagers living along the railway tracks, including an area of 10 kilometers on both sides of the tracks between Hohhot and Baotou on the Jingbao line. Baotou was considered a key village to provide protection. The stationmaster was assigned to serve as the chief of this Airo area.

Departing from Zhangjiakou, Maidazhao Station was one station before Salaqi. It was an especially rough area. The station staff protected the villagers and the villagers in turn did everything they could to protect the railway.

In Salaqi, the railway staff working for the Airo area was called the "railway team."

Under my father who was the stationmaster, Sergeant Okada of Military Police Subdivision and his staff of twenty members were working railroad security and for pacification of the rebellion.

Maidazhao Station was a relay station for trains that required coal supplies. It accommodated a large number of workers comprised of dispatch workers in charge of that railroad section, the electrical team of the railway maintenance division, and security staff.

The area around the station was one of the best opium-growing districts, and rock salt was abundant in nearby areas as well. The station bustled with workers carrying these products. The majority of the station passengers were rock salt carriers.

In fact, this area was part of a smugglers' route nearly 50 kilometers from the Yellow River. All types of people passed through. It was also a hotbed of fundraising for soldiers of China's Eighth Route Army.

During the 45 minutes it took for a train to be supplied with water and coals at Maidazhao Station, the rock salt carriers hid opium among the coals, or inside the oil cans that had been used as coal beds. The station overlooked the activity, and charged the carriers overseeing fees.

This income from the overseeing fees was about three times higher than the income from ticket sales for all the trains that came and went 16 times a day. It was a truly significant amount of money.

The entire amount of this miscellaneous income was divided between the military police, the consulate, the police station, and the local patrol team. It paid for the security of Maidazhao Station.

One day, Lieutenant Sasaki, who was the assistant to Lieutenant-Colonel Yamanaka, Chief of the Military Police Headquarters, traveled from Zhangjiakou to visit my father.

My father had taught judo to the military policemen in Zhangjiakou when he was an assistant stationmaster four years before. Lieutenant Sasaki said that those who had obtained black belt ranks were serving as squad leaders and performing greatly, and he, for starters, wanted to express his appreciation.

He then continued to say that the Japanese Imperial Army fighting in the south was not in great condition, and therefore the main divisions of the Kwantung Army were dispatched to the south one by one. His division, the 26th in Mongolia, had been ordered to move to the south.

The 26th Division was the team of soldiers who gave my sister a ride on their military truck singing heartily, *"Ame furi otsuki san, kumo no kage"* (Mr. Moon in the rain, behind the clouds) amid tears of nostalgia. They would later leave Datong for Luzon Island.

They fought on Leyte Island, only to be annihilated.

As time passed, security along the railroad became insufficient, and as a result, more incidents of violence occurred in the area.

Lieutenant Sasaki said that he wanted to meet Huang Youngchang of the Chinese Eighth Route Army, the man who had dealt the Japanese Army a blow during the Battle of Wuyuan.

Huan Youngchang was an imposing figure, almost two meters tall. He had entered the walls of Salaqi Castle on his own from the main gate, and attacked the infantry station. He captured the watch guards, backups, and soldiers who had just returned from patrol, more than ten men altogether, stripped off their uniforms, tied them in a row, and left, taking away their military uniforms, weapons, and ammunition.

The Japanese Army suffered a crushing defeat in the Battle of Wuyuan.

Lieutenant Sasaki wished to draw this dreaded figure into the Japanese Army to work for them, and had come to my father to make such an arrangement, saying, "Stationmaster, surely you can fulfill the role of a go-between."

My father immediately asked Bao Taibao who quickly agreed.

Huan Youngchang gave conditions: 40 to 50 local boys aged 14 to 17, each with weapons and ammunition so he could lead them as a battalion at war; arrange a military horse and both heavy and light automatic weaponry for himself; and to be treated as a major of an independent battalion commander of the Japanese Imperial Army.

The Japanese Army agreed to all of his demands.

His enrollment ceremony was conducted on the yard in front of Maidazhao Station with Military Police Captain Iwata in attendance.

Lieutenant Sasaki, my father as stationmaster, and Bao Taibao also attended. Huan Youngchang, mounted a horse and, accompanied by 50 teenage soldiers, combined for an imposing presence.

However, despite the agreement that he would be given the title of major of the independent battalion commander of the Japanese Imperial Army, he was entitled "Captain of an independent company of the Japanese Imperial Army." He complained.

Youngchang was appeased with the promise that he would later be appointed major, and on that note they ended the ceremony.

The situation in Maidazhao was such that my father arranged for his family to live in Hohhot while he lived alone and worked at Maidazhao Station.

He sometimes came home from Maidazhao, but during school holidays my mother visited him with all four children, staying in the stationmaster's living quarters. For us children, these short trips were our happiest times.

Bao Taibao never failed to visit us at Maidazhao Station. The

Maidazhao region was his home. He came to see his young lord. He was the guardian of the boy.

This role satisfied him enough to give up his plan to adopt the first son, but still, he was serious about adopting the second son. Whenever he saw my father, he repeated his appeal, saying that having two sons was unfair. He asked for one of them, promising that he would raise the boy to be a great man.

He always came with his henchmen carrying two sheep, ten chickens, and a basketful of chicken eggs. More henchmen appeared and quickly cooked them.

Bao Taibao would cut off some pieces of sheep meat with his knife and, with a smile, offered them to us children.

He also loved the omelet my mother cooked for children, and was curious to see *chawanmushi,* a Japanese cup of steamed egg custard containing vegetables and a ginkgo nut, among other foods.

The door was open at the stationmaster's quarters. Station staff and guards also joined them, giving the meeting a party atmosphere.

On the other hand, even though Bao Taibao appeared easygoing, still, he was the head of bandits. This powerful man was always on full alert, observing the moves of the station staff and people around him.

My father was totally relaxed when surrounded by his children.

In the summer night sky over this northern land, the Milky Way was wide and white like flowing milk. Stars that dotted the sky appeared to be an arm's length away.

Maidazhao was an extremely dangerous town, very different from Hohhot.

Gunshots were heard in the distance in the middle of the night. The elder son remained sound asleep, but the younger son startled with each shot. He was a sensitive boy, my father commented, not suitable to be brought up by a bandit.

In response, Bao Taibao said he could help the boy become a tough man. This strong-willed man never showed the slightest intention to give up.

No one knew how old Bao Taibao was. He himself did not know either. He seemed about ten years older than my father. He did not know where he was born, nor who his parents were. Since his earliest memories, he had been raised by bandits.

When we children came to see our father, Bao Taibao stayed at the station's living quarters with some of his henchmen to guard us. My father told him several times that it was unnecessary because there were military policemen, station guards, and the station crew, but Bao Taibao remained adamant that he was bodyguard to his young lord.

On regular days, on the other hand, he randomly appeared alone in the daytime. Such visits occurred as many as three or four times a week. His real purpose was to take a nap. The greatest problem for a leader of bandits was sleeping. He was active at night and could not sleep well in the daytime. He never knew when he might be betrayed. Any one of his henchmen could stab him in the back at any time. My father's stationmaster's living quarters was the safest place for him to nap.

The reason why my father chose to work in such a dangerous town as Maidazhao was because a master of Shaolin martial arts resided there. Wherever he was, my father always tried to find an opportunity to learn Chinese martial arts. Here in Maidazhao, he recruited Wang Kangren, a practitioner of Shaolin martial arts, to his station crew, lived with him around the clock and practiced with him.

Before the first train left the station before dawn, and after seeing off the last train of the day, the two devoted themselves to practicing. It was Bao Taibao who introduced Wang Kangren to my father. Sometimes the three practiced together. Bao Taibao was fairly skilled in the arts as well.

When my father was in Salaqi, he heard that there was an old master of Shaolin martial arts named Gengshen living deep in the Yin Mountains. He immediately journeyed to meet him. The master was a thin, frail figure, like a crane. Rather than a martial art master, he was more like an ascetic monk or hermit.

The old hermit completely won over my father's heart. After the visit, he managed to find time to visit the old man to receive his teachings.

The councilor of Salaqi, who was teaching judo at a school in Mongolia, had a high rank in Kodokan judo. He and my father immediately became good friends and visited each other to practice judo together.

....

The station crew at Maidazhao told my father that he was spending all his energy practicing karate and judo, and asked which was more important to him, his station tasks or his practice. "They both are important and they are not to be compared. However, I bear all responsibility on my shoulders for karate and judo. Please ensure that all the station staff cooperate and help each other to carry out their station duties," he answered very seriously.

Bao Taibao

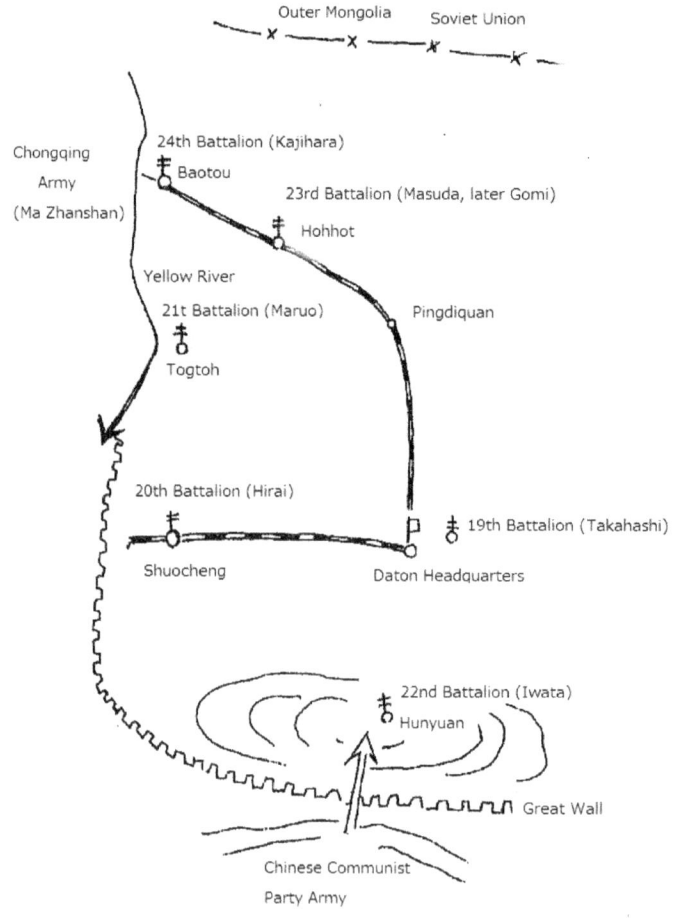

From around the spring of 1945, attacks by the rebels and bandits intensified.

Maidazhao, where my father was the stationmaster, and Salaqi, had originally been poor in public security. The troops led by Ma Zhanshan, another led by Fu Zuoyi, and the Eighth Route Army of the Chinese Communist Party, joined by bandits, were all dominant in these regions. Railroads were destroyed and the trains were attacked almost every day. At night, gunshots were constantly heard in the distance. Wondering when those guns would arrive at their doorstep, people tossed and turned at night.

The enemy army had already noticed that their Japanese adversaries were getting the worst of the war, but our Japanese Army, steeped in the notion they were invincible, never dreamed of such a situation.

In March, the Japanese Army in Mongolia established the headquarters of the 4th Independent Infantry Security Guard Divisions (Shisei Troops) in Datong. It formed six independent infantry troops whose main task was to guard the important places in Inner Mongolia and northern Shanxi Province.

The six divisions were assigned to suppress enemies and secure public safety in their respective areas.

However, the enemy attacks only grew more daring. By May, two out of six infantry divisions had their commanders themselves fight on the front lines of battles only to be shot by enemy snipers, worsening the situation.

Near death, one of the commanders, using his final reserves of energy, propped his bleeding body up with his sword to stand up with dignity and, looking up to the sky, declared, "May we win the Great East Asia War. Long live the Emperor. Long live the Emperor. Long… live…" He shouted and drew his final breath.

Deployment Map of the 4th Independent Infantry Security Guard Troops

Of course, along with the commanders, many soldiers died in the battles. Their friends desperately scrambled to gather their corpses under the cover of darkness during lulls in enemy fire.

Inner Mongolia, and northern Shanxi Province, where Shisei Troops were guarding, especially in Maidazhao and Salaqi, were hotbed regions for the cultivation of opium-producing poppy plants.

On the soil that had absorbed countless liters of blood spilled in battles throughout the ages, large poppy flowers bloomed red, white, and pink. It was a bumper crop, more beautiful than other years, covering the land as far as the eye could see, offering a spectacular view.

Around Maidazhao Station, the Eighth Route Army's attacks on the railroad intensified.

To cope, it was decided to surround the station building with an earthen wall to provide a bunker space to hide when towing locomotives. However, before carrying out the construction, my father distributed the money allocated by the railroad maintenance office to the military police and the station guards. He also gave away opium and cigarettes he had been given to native villagers to obtain enemy information from them.

One night, Lieutenant-Colonel Sasaki stopped by Maidazhao Station.

As he drank with my father in the stationmaster's room, gunshots were suddenly heard.

Sasaki immediately stood up and held up his gun. Not toward the gunshots outside, but toward my father.

Astonished, my father asked, still sitting.

"What's wrong?"

"Huan Youngchang has betrayed the Japanese Army!"

For an instant, my father could not understand what Lieutenant-Colonel Sakaki had said.

To Sasaki who was standing firmly with a gun in hand, my father repeated the same question. "What's wrong?"

"Huan Youngchang has betrayed us, the Japanese Army!" With full anger, Sasaki answered loudly.

"What! Then, why didn't you tell me?"

"Stationmaster, you really didn't know that?"

"If I had known that, I could have done something about it," my father said, remembering Bao Taibao's face.

It was my father who had introduced Huan Youngchang to the Japanese Army in the first place. If he had had the chance to discuss the defection with Bao Taibao, he could have stopped the betrayal of Huan Youngchang. Or so he thought at that time.

In retrospect, Huan Youngchang had carried out what had been planned from the start.

"We guessed you had known that. Actually, I came this evening to spy on your movements," Sasaki confessed.

Had my father said or done something that aroused Sasaki's suspicions, he would have been shot and killed on the spot for treason.

"Ridiculous! I am Japanese. I would never forgive anyone who betrays the Japanese Army."

He had already been thinking that he should clearly divide friends and foes. That was necessary at any time, but especially for those living on that land at that time. Knowing friend and foe was a matter of life and death. Even if he was on very good terms with someone in everyday life, he might have to fight against him if he took on the role of enemy.

Even without discussing such matters, Bao Taibao and my father had always fully understood that they would someday fight against each other and they were prepared for the day to come. When that day came, they would not hesitate or show mercy but fight fiercely but fairly against each other.

Nothing could change the fact that they were from different countries that were squared off against each other.

At dawn of the following day, Captain Huan Youngchang and his selected 50 boy soldiers who had gone through one-year of training, with weapons and ammunition provided by the Japanese Army, fled toward the mountains that glowed in the morning sun.

From the very next day, night raids began.

The gunshots heard when Lieutenant Sasaki visited my father were also the signal to begin an attack.

On that day, Bao Taibao disappeared.

A few days later, Lieutenant-Colonel Sasaki was attacked with a grenade that exploded and ripped open his chest. Sasaki laid dying on the square in front of the station.

After this loss, my father was seen with suspicion by the Japanese Army. Meanwhile, China's Eighth Route Army put a price on his head.

A few days later, at dawn on July 13th, Maidazhao Station where my father was working was violently attacked and completely destroyed.

The evening before that attack, my father had been invited to a dinner party for the military police. A messenger came to him during the party to tell him that the native assistant stationmaster on the night shift was absent. As the stationmaster, he had no choice other than filling his subordinate's role even though he had planned to go back to return to Hohhot to see his family after the party. It had been a long time since he last saw them. My father was in the dark regarding what was about to transpire.

When darkness fell, one Chinese station staff member casually strolled to the end of the platform, lit a cigarette, and blew a smoke ring upwards. Responding to this signal, a volley of fire rose along the Yin Mountains blackened by the night. Meanwhile, shadowy figures began to make their move.

Shortly after the gunshots heard in the evening ceased, my father felt sufficient relief to drift off to sleep.

Sleep was short-lived, however, as attackers kicked down his door and burst into his room, literally surprising him in bed. My father sprung up in a flash and instantaneously delivered a blow that gave him a chance to escape outside. When others jumped at him from both sides, he delivered roundhouse kicks to move further away, scramble over the railroad fence and run for his life into the darkness.

A bullet whistled over his head. That was followed by a volley of gunfire.

As he crouched and crawled into total darkness, he saw a flash of light in the distance over the water tower. As he gazed carefully, dark figures gathered around a small light and then hurriedly dispersed. It appeared that there was a commander standing at the center of a gathering of what looked like a shadow play.

He remembered an embankment behind them and decided to find a way to escape into it. If he could place himself right under the commander, he would be safe. As the saying goes, "The darkest place is under the candlestick."

In the darkness, he felt his way on the ground little by little while avoiding detection until he finally managed to sneak into the embankment.

He barely breathed while biding time.

Footsteps of people intent on killing him came and went above his head.

Hurried footsteps of someone approached, something was reported, the commander gave him an order, and the footsteps were gone.

Then suddenly, he heard a familiar voice.

"Our target is the stationmaster only. His head has a price. Leave everyone else alone."

It was Bao Taibao! That was unmistakable. Alas, the commander was his old friend.

Oppressive time dragged on.

Even though it was July, night on the Mongolian highlands was cold. Lying on the ground, the coldness gradually spread throughout his body and to the outermost reaches of his toes and fingertips. Over time he began to feel a sharp pain in the center of his backbone.

Each second felt like eternity.

He wondered how much time had passed. Would time stop there forever? Just when he began to feel night would never end, the whole sky brightened. That was followed by a very heavy noise that shook the ground.

The station building was completely destroyed.

The bombing produced a red fire, then black smoke. It was consumed in flames.

An armored train with troops returning from an assignment in Baotou noticed trouble at Maidazhao Station.

My father's judo friend happened to be on board as the train driver. My father and he were quite close; when they were working together in Zhangjiakou, they practiced intensively together in the judo club. Even after my father was transferred to Salaqi and Maidazhao as stationmaster, this friend occasionally visited him and enjoyed listening to his stories of heroism.

The engineer found the smoke rising up faintly ahead in the direction of the rising sun. It looked to be coming from Maidazhao Station. He immediately tried to contact the station, but the electricity wire had already been cut off. There was no way to directly contact the station. He then contacted the Zhangjiakou Railway Office via Salaqi Station, the station next to Maidazhao.

News of the raid on Maidazhao Station was immediately passed from the Zhangjiakou Railway Office to Hohhot Station, and on to my mother.

"Madam, I am sorry to disturb you at such an early hour. Please pack your things."

My mother instantly thought of my father.

"Something happened to my husband?"

"No clear information yet, but we heard that Maidazhao Station was attacked."

She was told to prepare for the worst.

On hearing there had been a raid, the face of Bao Taibao instantly appeared in my mother's mind.

There would be no one other than Bao Taibao who would attack that station. She remembered his slender and flexible body like a leopard, and his sharp eyes always alertly watching in every direction, even while laughing and eating.

Bao Taibao fulfilled the role of chief of the security guard in the Maidazhao region in the daytime, but given his background as head of the mounted bandits, it was only natural for him to assume that role in the nighttime.

His demeanor of alertness and readiness displayed no vulnerabilities.

Compared to Bao Taibao's attitude of extreme caution, my easygoing father was innocent and trusting, never refusing those who came to him and never chasing after those who went their own way. For warm-heartedness, Bao Taibao was no match for him.

Besides, the local Chinese staff at Maidazhao were all recruited by Bao Taibao.

My mother had repeatedly warned my father to be very careful, but he did not listen. While various thoughts and misgiving stirred in her mind, she felt more and more angry and uneasy.

Looking up to dawn breaking in the eastern sky, she prayed toward the direction of Maidazhao for the safety of my father.

Just after the black sky over the mountains changed its color to dark blue, a pale red streak appeared. That was the time Bao Taibao withdrew his band of followers.

Bao Taibao never turned back to see the embankment under him.

After the sound of footsteps faded away, my father slowly began to move and then crawled out.

The roof of the station building had been terribly burned, with some places still smoldering. The station staff and security guards who had been hiding in and around the water tower came out one by one and gathered around the stationmaster. They all checked the safety of each other.

The rebels even entered into the water tower brandishing guns, but when they understood that the stationmaster was not there, they left without harming the others. There were no casualties.

All the guns and ammunition, as well as a large amount of money and station supplies, had been taken away, but having lost no human lives was a blessed relief.

However, the local Chinese staff who they had been working with until the night before had all disappeared.

From the distance in the morning mist, they heard the sound of military horses approaching. A man in military garb was speaking loudly.

"Look at you, what a disgrace! Where is the stationmaster? Where is he?!"

Upon seeing my father the officer continued, "Stationmaster, what were you doing? You should commit *seppuku*!"

He was crazily shouting on the horse while circulating around my father and the station staff like a vulture. Behind him were the ruins of the bombed station.

His angry shouts echoed mournfully as the morning sun pulled away from the horizon.

He might have not just been blaming my father, but also expressing his own regret for being unable to protect it.

My father spoke to the officer on the horse.

"We were outnumbered."

My father then made all the staff line up and commanded, "Salute to Company Commander!"

The Japanese Army's defeat was only one month away.

Soviet Union Entrance

Maruichi Battle Position

On August 9th, 1945, the Soviet Union invaded northern Manchuria and the Mengjiang region of northern China, violating the Japanese-Soviet Non-Aggression Pact.

They advanced aggressively. The overwhelming military power of the Soviet Army quickly caused the withdrawal of the Kwantung Army who only protected their families then ran away. The Japanese residing in Manchuria were left behind to endure the local Mongolian mobs who rampaged the town, looting and committing acts of violence. If they survived that, capture by the Soviet Army would force them to later endure the severest hardships imaginable.

Among the Japanese in the region, pioneers residing in Manchuria's inland were not even informed of Japan's defeat despite that fact that immigration to Manchuria had been national policy.

The proud Kuwantang Army, which had fancied themselves invincible, had sent the majority of its soldiers south, and consequently were left with virtually no defense. In any case, it was a miserable, disgraceful end.

Compared to that chaos, those of us who were beyond the Great Wall in the Huabei and Mengjiang regions were very lucky even though remoteness had its own drawbacks. The "luck" we enjoyed was entirely made possible by Commander Hiroshi Nemoto and the Mongolia Garrison Army.

Since his arrival as the commander of the Mongolia Garrison Army at the end of 1944, Lieutenant General Hiroshi Nemoto had been concerned about the threat posed to areas bordering the Soviet Union.

Therefore, at news of the Soviet invasion, he ordered to have the Japanese who had been in Hohhot and more inner areas gather in Zhangjiakou to arrange evacuations to less dangerous places.

Without the quick and accurate decision of this commander, we can only imagine what fate we would have endured. If we had evacuated after August 15th, the day of Japan's unconditional surrender, being far inland would have made our withdrawal from the continent very difficult. Worse, I wonder if we could have been evacuated at all.

Indeed, after our evacuation, the railroad bridge and the communication line between Zhangjiakou and Datong were destroyed. Evacuees from Datong were forced to endure extreme hardship making a

Soviet Union Entrance

detour via Taiyuan.

Our lives had quickly became desperate.

My sister in the second-grade vividly remembers her last day at school in Hohhot, the farewell words exchanged with her teacher, and her school report cards and notebooks distributed in the class, as if it was only yesterday.

On that day, children hastily went home with air raid hoods covering their heads.

On August 11th, we were told to withdraw from Hohhot, but we still had not heard word from father. When my mother finally got to Hohhot Station, and asked the station staff to let her use the railway phone, she could hear his voice. He had been extremely busy with train arrangements for Japanese residents to gather in Zhangjiakou. After that we finally reunited.

Before packing up our belongings, he quickly brought a Chinese neighbor and told him that he could have all the items left in the house and the hens in the henhouse on condition that the neighbor roast three or four chickens immediately. The Chinese family happily agreed to those terms.

Thanks to the deal, we packed whole roasted chickens as well as dozens of boiled eggs for our journey. My father's priority was always food for his children. He made sure never to let his children experience hunger.

A short time later, we residents of Hohhot and those from more inner areas gathered in Zhangjiakou.

In Zhangjiakou, Kahoku Traffic Company provided us their girls' dormitory to stay. We could watch the giant sun set on Zhangjiakou once more from the second story balcony.

My mother was familiar with Zhangjiakou; she had many memorable moments there. It was the first town in the Mengjiang region where she lived after traversing a great distance and crossing over the Great Wall. And it was where I and the long awaited first son were born. Mother could relax there as if she had returned to her hometown.

Moreover, my mother was expecting her fifth baby.

Upon arrival, she had thought we would stay in Zhangjiakou for an extended period, but even the inner region was becoming unsafe with the invasion of the Soviet army. She had not imagined that Japan's defeat was imminent.

In fact, she knew nothing about the Emperor's announcement, made at noon on August 15th, 1945. People tried to listen on the radio but it was too noisy to understand what was being said.

However, the atmosphere of the town was unusual. She had heard a rumor that Japan had lost the war, and gradually it became clear that it was not a rumor, but Japan had actually been defeated.

At the headquarters of the Mongolia Garrison Army, Commander Nemoto refused to disarm even after the unconditional surrender. He was determined to do anything to stop the Soviet invasion and get the Japanese staying in Zhangjiakou, Beijing, Tianjin and elsewhere back home safely. To that end, a division of the Mongolia Garrison Army was allocated to the Maruichi Battle Position in Zhangbei where the Japanese Army had had an outpost aiming to stop incoming rebels.

There was one problem with Nemoto's plan. Since Japan had already surrendered unconditionally, refusing to disarm meant he was opposing the command of the Emperor. In that way, Commander Nemoto risked his life to protect Japanese citizens and soldiers of the Mongolia Garrison Army and save them from the purgatory—or more likely hell—of captivity in a Soviet gulag.

On August 17th, my mother went to the supply store of Zhangjiakou Station. There were no odd moves in the town, but the atmosphere had changed somewhat. The Material Division staff remembered my mother very well.

"Of course I know you. When the assistant stationmaster's son was born... Um... He is a stationmaster now, isn't he? We still talk about how excited he was when his son was born. It's the most exciting thing that ever happened in Zhangjiakou!"

After catching up on their lives and concerns for the future, my mother bought some glutinous rice and red beans to cook *seki-han*, a celebratory red rice dish. Luckily, the Materials Division still had plenty of food left.

The following day was my younger brother's birthday. My mother did not know how we would live in the future, but she wanted to at least

Soviet Union Entrance

celebrate my brother's birthday like any other year.

On August 18th, the following day, my mother unpacked the baggage brought from Hohhot, and in the yard of the girls' dormitory, their temporary residence provided by Kahoku Traffic Company in Zhangjiakou, she brought out a warrior doll and war helmet for the Boys' Festival, and a *hina* doll prince and princess and placed them on a tiered *hina* stand made especially for *hina* dolls.

We celebrated my little brother's birthday, Boys' Festival, and Girls' Festival all at the same time.

We siblings were excited, helping my mother display the dolls and make rice balls with the *seki-han*, placing a few in front of the dolls as offerings.

My younger brother, the birthday boy, kept smiling shyly. According to the age counting custom of those days, we added the year the developing babies spent in their mother's womb. Thus, he turned three, but by today's custom he would have just turned two years old.

We were all happy with the celebratory dishes my mother had lovingly prepared. We sang songs, chatted, and laughed together. Knowing the family could take very few possessions, my mother had a surprise that also served as a lesson in impermanence. After the merry party ended, she called us to the yard, and said with a flourish, "Let's say farewell to the warrior, the prince and the princess!" She then promptly set them on fire. We children were all dumbfounded. This was an ironic twist of tradition, an alternative to sending the hina dolls afloat down the river, an act which was believed to cast off the sorrows and tribulations of the girls they had belonged to.

That night, I was having a hard time falling asleep. The images were still vivid in my mind: the destruction of the crimson-carpeted *hina* stand, the prince and princess dolls being dropped into the fire, the mighty warrior doll engulfed in flames, and the *seki-han* rice balls rolling off the decorative stand.

Now wide awake, I wondered what happened to them after that, as if they could have survived the fire.

As I sat up quietly, my sister, who seemed to also be replaying the day's events, sat up and said, "I am going to go see them."

"*You* is going, too," I said, calling myself '*you*' as was my habit since infancy.

"No, you stay in bed."

"No, *you*—meaning "I"—want to go too."

"Will you be a good girl?"

"Yes, *you* (I) will be good."

The two brothers were sound asleep curled up in seahorse postures. They were facing each other, as if happily carrying on a conversation in their dreams.

My sister and I snuck out of the room without making a sound. The burned dolls were neatly swept into a corner of the yard. In front of them was our mother standing still holding a broom and dustpan.

Then she sat down and with both hands she began to stroke her bulging belly containing another baby that would soon make its entrance into the world. While gently stroking her stomach she gazed into the distance.

I wonder what she was thinking at that moment.

We lost our *hina* dolls to flames twice; the first time was in the fire caused by the overheated stovepipe at Kahoku Traffic's company housing on Dong'an Street, not far from where we now stood watching our mother.

The second time was again here in Zhangjiakou, the finale to our great celebration. My mother had had to burn them with her own hands this time. The *Hina Matsuri*, the Girls Festival, was originally an event to offer up the sins and calamities of daughters to the gods, with the *hina* dolls acting as substitutes for human females.

If she had been thinking of that, she might have been praying to the dolls in the fire, asking them to protect her daughters from the hardships that would begin the very next day.

After a while, she started to sing slowly in a low voice. It was the *Hina Matsuri* song.

> *Shall we light the paper lanterns?*
> *Shall we display peach flowers?*

Her thin and tender voice rose quietly into the night sky of Zhangjiakou, the waxing moon nearly full.

Two days later, the full withdrawal of Japanese soldiers and civilians from Zhangjiakou began.

Total Repatriation

Zhangjiakou Station

Two days later, Japanese total repatriation started in Zhangjiakou.

We had the great fortune to avoid the tragedy that those who were trapped in Inner Manchuria experienced, but still, total withdrawal from the continent caused great confusion and strife.

An announcement was made telling us to gather immediately with minimal personal belongings. Responding to the order, many of us hurried to the station and were made to board the repatriation trains, never having the chance to return to the beloved houses where we had been living.

This regret gnawed at people for a long time thereafter.

We all longed to return to our homes and take at least one or two treasured possessions. However, this was the best that the Mongolia Garrison Army and Kahoku Traffic company could do. Total repatriation would require preparation time and evacuees would want to carry more and more possessions.

Even in such a crisis, there were some who had realized that repatriation was imminent. Baggage was brought and piled up in front of the station. The area was crowded with Japanese who were reluctant to leave their possessions and the Chinese there eager to take home whatever we couldn't bring.

A fire broke out in front of the crowd. The Japanese hotel *Hiroshima Ryokan* was on fire. The owner had gone through various hardships earlier in her life. She finally arrived in Zhangjiakou and started managing that hotel. She had taken very good care of the soldiers of the Mongolia Garrison Army, treating them like her own children.

Now that we had lost the war, the woman lost everything and had nowhere to go. So she changed into a formal black kimono and started the fire herself. In the blazing flames, the view of the white socks of the black kimono-clad owner scurrying up the stairs to her death was a vivid memory.

People were not aware of it, but around that time the tanks of the Soviet Union Army had already arrived at the Maruichi Military Position north of Zhangjiakou.

The Mongolia Garrison Army and Kahoku Traffic decided to implement the total repatriation of the 40,000 Japanese gathered in Zhangjiakou to Beijing and Tianjin in three days, from August 20th.

Total Repatriation

During this time "Hibiki Heidan," the second independently combined brigade of the Mongolian Army, was formed to stop the Soviet Union Army from advancing into Zhangjiakou. They were initially stationed at the Maruichi Battle Position.

Some call it a miraculous escape of the 40,000 Japanese, as if a *kamikaze*, a divine wind, blew us all safely back to our homeland, but it was no such thing. Rather, it was made possible by a large number of people who risked their lives to protect us.

The Kahoku Traffic staff operated the repatriation trains without any sleep or rest. They exclusively used all the cargo trains with and without roofs to carry the Japanese evacuees. Even then, arranging enough trains was not easy.

Kesanosuke Ishii of the Industry Division of the Mengjiang government, the consulate office in China, had bought supplies in Tianjin. Just before sending them to Mengjiang on August 9th, he heard about Japan's unconditional surrender on a shortwave radio broadcast. He immediately rerouted the 150 cargo trains which were to send goods to Mengiang, and instead redirected the empty trains to Zhangjiakou.

This courageous emergency measure allowed those trains to serve as precious vehicles for human cargo, and the supplies Mr. Ishii did not send to Zhangjiakou greatly helped the Japanese in Tianjin.

Mr. Ishii also worked with the Mengjiang government making their best efforts for the passengers on repatriation trains arriving in Zhanjiakou, arranging food at Xizhimen, a gate to Beijing's city wall. They had the wives of Japanese government officers residing in Beijing make rice balls, and bought a large quantity of flatbreads from Chinese sellers, paying much money. For three days and nights, they distributed these foods to people on the trains who were arriving in droves.

The majority of the passengers were on trains without roofs under miserable conditions, exposing them all to the hot sun and rain. With my mother expecting another baby at the end of the month, my family was placed in the group of those who were ill or pregnant, riding on a train with a roof. Even in a roofed car, the journey must have been hard beyond description to my pregnant mother who was tending to the needs of four small children.

For fear of attacks and sabotage at night, the trains ran only in the daytime. After the sun set, people stayed at schools, temples, or the dormitories of young men's associations along the railroad tracks. They then made rice balls and came back on board at sunrise. The tracks were bombed several times, requiring repairs Each time the trains and passengers were forced to wait.

Traveling from Zhangjiakou to Beijing usually took about seven hours, but during the repatriation it took two days. Then after a four-day trip from Beijing we arrived in Tianjin, a city much closer to the coast and boats that would take us back to Japan, in a pouring rain.

My pregnant mother always carried the items she would need for childbirth while carrying her youngest son on her back.

In such weather, we were carried by truck to a Japanese national school that served as our camp. Many people had been brought there from different regions. In classrooms and the lecture hall, people circled their belongings to claim and secure their territory. The space inside the circles constituted the family's living space. Of course, everyone wanted to have as much space as possible. The bigger the family, the wider the territory claimed.

Among those who had traveled in the open-air train car, some had gotten soaking wet in the rain or were splattered with mud, causing them to fall ill. Japanese doctors were treating such people. My pregnant mother had gone in and out of trucks and had gotten caught in the rain as well. She soon arranged to see one of the doctors.

As her due date was fast approaching, she was told to wait for delivery in another building. It used to be the living quarters of that school's principal, a large Japanese-style house in a quiet, one could even say perfect, environment. Some other women were waiting to give birth as well.

Doctors and nurses were on standby with the baby bath ready. While the infants were to be waited on hand and foot, the mothers who would bear them had to do everything on their own.

In those days, there were still Japanese residents in Tianjin. We received great assistance from the local ladies' club who distributed food and clothing.

Early the following morning, my mother gave birth in the guest room with a *tokonoma*—a space in a traditional Japanese room for displaying a scroll and other ornaments.

In the middle of the chaos of the repatriation, the birth of a new life was a light of hope, and at the same time, a great responsibility for my mother to bear. In fact, she felt tremendous pride knowing that she was just as dedicated to this new life as the others, despite the circumstances. The order of being born first or second was not an issue. Every life could just emerge into this world one time. Besides, although she was living through a crisis, the baby did not choose when to come out.

Later in life, my mother sometimes remembered and talked about the hardship she had endured during the repatriation, but when she talked about the birth of her youngest child, she lit up with joy.

This last child was born with the support and protection of many people. My baby sister was not only mother's, but rather a child of society, or even, of the world. The kanji for her name *Kimiko*, contained the radicals of both "public" and "child."

Everyone showered my cute little sister with affection and lovingly raised her to be a sweet girl in accordance with my mother's wishes.

"The baby has been born. Let's go see her," my sister said. She stood up holding the hands of my two brothers. Now she fulfilled the role of guardian for the boys in place of our mother.

I hastily said, "*You* is going. Take *you*, too," still calling myself 'you', and tried to follow. But she firmly said, "No, you stay home. Watch our area, okay?"

Left alone, I sat in the middle of our territory surrounded by our baggage with a big pouty face.

After a while, a man with gray-streaked hair emerged from the baggage circle next to ours. I hadn't noticed anyone there. He suddenly sat up and little by little pushed his baggage toward our area.

At first, I did not understand what was happening. As I watched, he pushed his belongings even more.

Oh, no! He was attempting to expand his territory. I was instructed to watch our area. I had to protect our territory.

I said, "No, no!" to the man, almost crying, and tried my best to push his baggage back.

The man glared at me severely. His demeanor displaying either surprise or disgust, as if saying, "You cheeky child!" He turned his back to me and laid on the floor again on the other side of the baggage.

Meanwhile, opposite our territory, a man spread a Japanese flag on his lap and stroked it gently, saying "Why did we lose? Why did we lose? Didn't the *kamikaze* wind blow?" He was weeping.

"The baby was so cute!"
"Yes, she was really cute."
"Oh yes, very cute, very very cute."
My sister and brothers came back smiling happily.

Three days after my mother's delivery, my family moved to a Japanese hotel in connection with Kahoku Traffic.

Each family settled in respective guest rooms. It was decided that the large kitchen was to be shared by each family in turn. We could live a relaxed life among family members for the first time since we hurriedly left home.

There were large sofas and chairs for socializing piled up in one corner of the hotel's entrance. That place immediately became our playground. We jumped on the soft sofas or sat quietly playing "Cat's Cradle," making string figures with yarn. My younger brother followed me everywhere I went.

The Imperial Portrait Train

Datong Station

Ten days had passed before my father became aware of the fact that the war had ended.

Considering the series of events—the raid on Maidazhao Station, the Soviet Union Army's entry into the war followed by the immediate withdrawal of Japanese residents living in inner areas and my father's own family being sent from Hohhot to Zhangjiakou—one would think that Japan's imminent defeat was perfectly clear. Despite all that, my father had failed to see the obvious.

In fact, he had never for a moment thought Japan's defeat a possibility.

However terrible the war situation was, however desperate, he firmly believed that our Imperial Army would reverse the tide and win the war.

The Mongolia Garrison Army governed Kahoku Traffic as its transportation division in northern China. The army and company staff collaborated during the war.

My father was assigned to take charge of train transport of the Imperial Army. That included the special train carrying a *goshinei*, a portrait of the emperor who was revered as a living God.

The engine pulled three roofed cars. The first and the third cars protected the second car carrying the imperial portrait. The imperial portrait was guarded by one second lieutenant, two sergeants, one senior soldier, one first-class private, and two privates.

They were ready for combat.

My father was requested to be on board to guard this train.

The railroad condition between Baotou and Hohhot had become worse with more frequent attacks on trains and sabotage of tracks. Whenever the engine got damaged, the train got stuck for a while. The train struggled along, got repaired before incurring damage again, then finally managed to arrive at Datong Station.

As leader, my father stopped the train at platform 8 and told the major guarding the imperial portrait to wait while he got some food. The major angrily replied to forget about food in such an emergency and get the train running again immediately.

But as the saying goes, "An army marches on its stomach." My father explained that everyone on the train had not eaten a meal for two days. The train driver desperately needed some food. Without nutrition, the

The Imperial Portrait Train

imperial portrait was vulnerable to attack. The truth was that the young driver and soldiers who were forced to stand straight and stiff to fend off attacks needed food. So my father prevailed, telling the major to wait while he left to get food.

Datong Station was a familiar station where he once worked as assistant stationmaster. However, he sensed something was wrong.

It was then that he was informed for the first time that the war had ended.

Moreover, he was not told by the Japanese Army but by Yan Xishan's Army of the National Government of the Republic of China, the enemy. A military officer of Yan Xishan's Army, whose rank was unknown but seemed high ranking, politely received my father. He stood straight, and told my father that the Japanese Imperial Army had unconditionally surrendered on August 15th.

"Impossible!" my father cried out in disbelief. It felt as if all energy drained out of his body. Having been so certain of Japan's eventual victory, his mind could not fully process this news. The officer then told him something totally unexpected.

"It has been a long time since I last saw you. I sincerely welcome you here."

And then, to the soldiers around him, "This is my good friend," he said.

"No, rather he is my lifesaver. On this desk inside Datong Station, he gave me his box lunch," he added.

My father then recalled that incident.

Yes, that freeloader he encountered that day was not an ordinary man as he had presumed. He had risen to become a senior officer of the Yan Xishan's Army.

The officer softly said, "Please do not worry. I will have food prepared for you. Please take a rest before eating."

However, the *goshinei* train carrying the imperial portrait would not wait. Urged by the second lieutenant guarding the portrait, the train pulled out of the station without my father.

A short time later on the Datong Yuhe Railway Bridge, bombs struck it, blowing the imperial portrait train and nearby cars up.

"Hibiki Heidan," the second independent combined brigade of the Mongolian Army, stopped the Soviet Union Army at the Maruichi Battle Position and helped the 40,000 Japanese who had gathered in Zhangjiakou escape the town in three days. They solemnly traversed the Badaling Great Wall and returned to Japan.

However, "Shisei Heidan," the fourth independent infantry brigade, guarding mainly Datong as well as Inner Mongolia and northern Shanxi Province, did not catch wind of the news of the war's end, partly due to damaged radio transmission. Thus, they were left behind in the far-away western region. Besides, the iron bridge between Datong and Zhangjiakou had been destroyed, cutting off the return route for the 20,000 Japanese who had escaped from inner regions.

Datong, with the headquarters of the kempei-tai, was completely occupied by Yan Xishan's Army.

Shanxi Province was originally ruled by the faction to which Yan Xishan belonged. After returning to his homeland in high spirits, Yan Xishan brought hardships down onto the Japanese.

First, certain Japanese personnel were made to remain. In Datong, huge coal reserves remained buried underground. Hoping to continue developing this industry, he forced Japanese engineers to stay along with medical staff.

Also, the Datong troops of the Japanese Army were ordered by the Chinese Nationalist Government Army to join the war against the Communist Party Army.

With their war over, the Japanese wanted to go home as soon as possible. However, they were forced to remain with the promise that Yan Xishan would guarantee the repatriation of the First Troops of the Japanese Army and the Japanese citizens remaining in Datong.

Xishan would not let one single Japanese go home unless other Japanese agreed to stay. This demand by Yan Xishan, agreed to by the senior officers of the Japanese Army, could not be refused. Thus, even after orders for demobilization had taken effect, Japanese who longed to go home were forced to stay.

After all, these Japanese soldiers had fought for almost four years with the Datong Troops of the Datong Remaining Special Mission Corps. Many of them fought and died heroically in an effort to stop the takeover of Datong by the Communist Party Army. They were finally defeated by the overwhelming strength of the enemy.

After surrender, they were captured by the Communist Party Army, and taken as prisoners of war. While some of them could return to Japan after a few years, others including Major Ushinosuke Gomi, the 22nd battalion commander, died in prison, never to set foot on their homeland again.

Also, they were repeatedly invited to join the Eighth Route Army of the Chinese Communist Party and remain on the continent. In such cases, Japanese members of the Communist Party in Chinese military garb came to them and persuaded them to stay saying that returning to a defeated country would not be a good idea. Finding food and a place to live in a country so devastated by war would be difficult, but if they joined the Communist Party they would be respected and treated well.

However, those who responded to the invitation of Japanese members of the Chinese Communist Party and returned to Zhangjiakou were betrayed by Japanese Communists, charged with war crimes, and shot dead in front of the statue of Prince Kitashirakawa on the bank of the Qinghe River.

After the imperial portrait train was bombed, the senior officer of Yan Xishan's Army offered my father bodyguards to accompany him from Datong Station to Tianjin. However, my father could not accept the offer. There were Japanese who had escaped from the inner areas to Datong and were left behind. He had to get them home. That was his duty.

My father asked the officer to cooperate.

There were cargo trains piled high with high quality coals in Datong Station. He wanted to distribute the coals to Chinese villagers to simultaneously empty the trains while making them available to carry Japanese on repatriation.

The officer immediately agreed.

The villagers along the railroad were all excited. They had never afforded such high quality black coals which seemed to glitter like gold. Allowed to take as many as desired, they went back and forth between the station and homes, leaving no coals on the trains.

These roofless empty trains were then designated to carry Japanese on repatriation from Datong.

When my father left Datong Station, the ex-freeloader turned high ranking officer arrived at the station, saluted my father formally, and stood there until my father left his field of vision.

Upon my father's arrival in Tianjin, surprised people said, "Oh, is that a ghost?" They squeezed his arms and legs to make sure he was flesh and blood.

News of the imperial portrait train bombing had already been transmitted to the Mongolia Garrison Army and Kahoku Traffic.

My father visited many camps including Awaji National School, Fuyo National School, and Butokuden Hall among others to find us. When he arrived at one particular school, he had the feeling of having been there before.

Yes, he remembered. At the time of the Langfang Incident, after spying Chinese rebels around Fengtai Station near the Marco Polo Bridge, he stayed at the Fuyo Hotel which was mainly used by the Japanese Army. The journalist staying in the room next door had held a lecture at this school.

When he began his speech with the fateful words: "If Japan gets involved with a war against the United States, there is no doubt that Japan will lose," he was ushered off the stage into captivity. This was the place where that had occurred, he realized without a doubt.

The following day, that contact man with the black glasses had hurriedly approached my father and repeatedly questioned him about whether he had been asked to keep something. He came to understand that the contact man had been talking about the speech the journalist had written. The journalist had been concentrating on his writing in the room next door and might have shared the lecture script. This was the contact man's concern.

The journalist could not express more than a word of his thoughts at the lecture. It must have been painful for him.

The contact man with black glasses was concerned about my father, wondering if he had received the script. However, the journalist did not give it to my father. He surely didn't want to get my father into any trouble. He was a good man, a true Japanese man. My father recalled his bright smile when he said he would like to see my father's martial art skill.

The place where the journalist was captured was now full of people on repatriation. The children were bouncing off the walls.

My father had finally managed to arrive at our hotel. When he spotted us, he was overjoyed. He picked up his infant daughter, his youngest child, cradled her in his arms, and held her tightly.

Puyi, Emperor of Manchukuo, had moved from the capital Hsinking to a temporary palace in Dalizi at the base of Mount Paektu after the invasion of the Soviet Union Army into Manchuria on August 9th.

There, on August 15th, he listened to the Emperor's announcement on the radio.

On August 18th, Puyi abdicated the throne. Manchukuo ceased to exist after 13 years and six months.

Puyi wished to exile to Japan. On August 20th, however, just before boarding the plane to Japan at Mukden Airport, he was captured by the Soviet Union Army and sent to Siberia where he was a prisoner of war for ten years before returning to China.

The South Manchuria Railway Co., Ltd. was dissolved due to capitulation. After the paperwork was processed, the company ceased to exist after a 39 year history.

The Great Tianjin Riot

Butokuden Hall

In October, the weather turned bitter cold.

Wanting to make a blanket to carry her baby on her back, my mother went to Tianjin to buy some fabric. If you had money, you could buy anything in that city.

To her great relief, she could use the Mengjiang currency. In Beijing and Tianjin, the bank notes used were those issued by the Federal Reserve Bank of China, but the Menjiang currency rate was higher.

At the end of the war, the Menjiang government returned all the deposits that the Bank of Menjiang had received to the depositors.

However, the Menjiang government and the Bank of Menjiang both dissolved after that. This seemed to mean that the bank notes issued by the Bank of Menjiang suddenly became worthless paper. But, as Inner Mongolia was a large opium-growing district, faith in currency issued by the Bank of Menjiang was maintained due to this cash crop.

The town was surprisingly quiet. After purchasing some large baked chestnuts and steamed buns for snacks, my mother stopped by a shop selling clothing and fabric. She also found various Western items to go with European dresses.

From among the assorted vividly-colored Chinese fabrics, my mother picked up a rather chic purple one with a pattern of large peony flowers spread all over in various shades of purple. The overall design was sublime.

My mother liked the idea of her baby wrapped in many peony flowers when she held her. That would be a splendid way to celebrate her birthday. Given their hectic lives at the camp, it wasn't easy to find the right birthday present. She wanted to go back immediately and start working on it.

Mother was about to leave the shop in a great mood, when it suddenly got noisy outside. The loud, angry voices of an approaching mob were becoming audible.

The shopkeeper stopped my mother from leaving.

A gang of 20 or 30 people carrying cloth, like handkerchiefs, or brandishing wooden sticks, were approaching, shouting something angrily.

The women of the group were in Korean clothing. Korean men and women had never dressed in their traditional clothing in the presence of the Japanese. They had even hidden their Korean ethnicity, but with Japan's defeat, they changed into Korean clothing and were marching boldly.

Just at that time, two former Japanese soldiers came plodding along from the opposite direction. Without hesitation, a few of the Koreans rushed at the soldiers and pushed one down to the ground, punching him. The other soldier tried his best to help and rescue his friend, repeatedly bowing his head to beg the Koreans for forgiveness. Then another Korean kicked the Japanese who showed no intention to fight back.

Voices from the Korean group told them to stop. The men scrambled to catch up with them. The former Japanese soldiers sat on the side of the road, unable to stand up for a while.

My mother was watching the whole scene from inside the shop.

Not long before, this sort of disorderly mob was unheard of. The Japanese soldiers might have been singing military songs while proudly marching in perfect unison: "We courageously march on with a promise of victory..."

Everyone had shown respect to the soldiers. These soldiers were presumed to be brave. When they were walking on the street, women and children would step aside to let them pass saying, "Make way for the soldiers!"

These proud and strong Japanese soldiers had turned into such weak figures overnight. The implications of the surrender turned the local power structure upside down. The Japanese had seemed invincible as a group, but on the individual level, they became weak in an instant.

After the rioters had gone, the shopkeeper told my mother that the immediate danger had passed, but the main street was not yet safe. To avoid any trouble, he told her about a back door exit behind the shop.

My mother was moved. She sincerely thanked him for saving a Japanese. He said appreciation was unnecessary because to him it did not matter at all whether she was Japanese, Chinese, or Korean. She had bought goods from his shop, so she was a customer. It was only natural for a shopkeeper to protect his customer. He told her to be careful on the way home.

Two days later, on October 13th, the situation deteriorated.

Mobs started a riot in Tianjin's Japan section.

It was on the day when the remaining Japanese residents in Tianjin received swords and guns from the underground. Local Koreans had probably caught wind of this arms distribution and attempted to take the weapons from the Japanese. This battle over arms had been the cause the riot.

Japanese unfortunate enough to have been walking on the street at that time were attacked by the mobs and killed one after another. A Japanese woman on a rickshaw was dragged down from the vehicle and beaten to death.

American soldiers were dispatched to quell the violence. They drenched the mobs with high pressure water hoses and took some away in their trucks.

On the day of this riot, my father was visiting the headquarters of Kahoku Traffic on East Chang'an Avenue of Beijing to submit a report on repatriation and to receive his monthly salary and retirement allowance. On his way back, as he got off the train at Tianjin North Station on the Pingchan line, he sensed something amiss. Someone was following him. It seemed there was not just one person. Two? Or three?

He immediately broke into a sprint, surprising his followers who then chased him.

My father ran up a path, turned some corners, and waited for them. He lost each of the three one by one, and then returned to the main street.

It was already dark.

On a desolate street, a Chinese soldier armed with a bayonet called out to my father and stopped him from behind.

"What country are you from? What is your nationality?" the soldier said. My father quickly answered, "I'm Mongolian."

"You are lying. I can tell by the way you walk."

"You know that by watching my feet?"

"Of course. Chinese, Mongolians, Japanese, Koreans, they all move differently." This observation immediately piqued my father's interest.

"Really? Then tell me, how do they differ? Could you show me?"

Carried on by my father's keen interest, the man showed him several walking styles: hold the hip high, stretch the knee and land with the heel, or bend the back and knees and land with a flat sole.

"Okay, then, how about turning, not walking forward? Please show me," my father asked.

"Splendid! Your footwork is awesome. You must be a devoted practitioner."

My father learned that the Chinese sentry's name was Shandong. With on-the-spot ad libs and demonstrations, they got deeply engrossed in their discussion about martial arts skills, karate forms and foot techniques.

After they finished their discussion and my father was walking away, Shandong came back to himself and his duty as a sentry. He shouted at my father, "Hey! Walk on the side of the road. Those from a defeated country are not entitled to walk in the middle!"

My father turned back and answered loudly: "You and I share the same passion for martial arts. There is no winner or loser between us! Besides, I am not a soldier who survived battles. I am walking in the middle of the road with my head high!"

The sentry responded, "I'm telling you for your own good! It's dangerous to walk in the middle."

Soon, the sentry's words proved true. Before he had walked far, my father was surrounded by a mob of people. Some of them were waving sticks. He did not know at that time about the riot that had occurred earlier that day. In fact, the unruly crowd had not completely cooled down since the riot, and were still restless to express dissatisfaction and hatred towards their former occupiers.

My father could have easily seized their sticks and given them a taste of their own medicine, but hitting people who did not know how to fight and possibly injuring them could cause a bigger problem.

He decided it was wiser to ignore them and escape the scene. He slipped his hand into his jacket as if he had a gun and, keeping track of the distance between himself and each potential assailant, he bolted out of this circle of menace. He handed money to the private gate guard at a large house, moved stealthily around the yard, jumped over the mud wall, opened the iron gate of the next house, and went to a rickshaw pool where drivers had gathered.

He got ahold of one of the rickshaw drivers, stuffed some cash into his hand, and instructed him to drive as if he had a customer while my father hid under the rickshaw.

As the rickshaw pulled away he could still hear angry voices shouting in the distance.

Meanwhile, at the hotel where we were staying, they closed the gate due to the riot. We were trapped inside. In the evening, we all waited for those who had gone out in the day to confirm that each one had returned safely.

Even as night fell, however, my father did not come back.

My mother kept knitting the baby blanket all night, anxiously waiting for him.

That had been always her way to cope. The night when Bao Taibao attacked Maidazhao Station, when the imperial portrait train was bombed, and again that night when the riot occurred in Tianjin, she took out her yarn and knitting needles. As she knitted to pass the time she prayed for my father's safe return.

Around her knees, her children were sound asleep with their heads huddled together in the shape of a fan.

When dawn came, my father silently got back.

At the end of the war, Chairman Chiang Kai-shek issued famous statements.

"We regard only the Japanese military as enemy, not Japanese citizens."

"Never blame the past. Instead, repay hostility with benevolence."

These statements impressed many people.

He also supported the repatriation of the Japanese.

This made it possible for us to gather in Tianjin and quickly withdraw to our homeland in an organized manner.

To pay back this favor, Lieutenant General Nemoto later secretly traveled under permission of Chairman Chiang Kai-shek and joined the Battle in Kinmen.

The U.S. Army provided us with LST—"Landing Ship, Tank"—ships to carry vehicles, cargo, and troops directly onto land. Our destination was, of course, Japan.

To assist Japan's repatriation efforts, the commander of the Mongolia

Garrison Army arranged and operated as many roofed and roofless trains as he could find. This was the same commander who saved many Japanese civilians at the risk of his own life while losing 81 soldiers at the Maruichi Battle Position and at Kahoku Traffic by leading the Hibiki troops to battle the invading Soviet Army. The Mengjiang Government provided all the materials and food they could.

What a large number of people heroically saved us!

The decisions made by these leaders changed the fate of many ordinary citizens. One leader's ability to take the appropriate action could save thousands or even tens of thousands of lives.

Just such a decision saved us from the abject misery experienced by those who got stuck in Manchuria.

At each camp, Japanese were waiting for their turn to get on a boat back to Japan.

We were staying in a Japanese hotel room used as a camp for a while. After the riot, the gate to the hotel was always closed. We heard that if a Japanese ventured outside of the gate and walked in the town, he would be quickly captured, never to return.

Even then, there were some who had to go out to buy food or essential goods, or to check the whereabouts of family or relatives they had lost on their way to the hotel.

Moreover, constant contact had to be maintained between each camp and repatriation headquarters. My father was often out for that purpose. He was the leader of our camp, taking care of everyone.

When going out, we quietly exited out of a small secret door. When we again opened the door upon returning, we were required to pull a rope dangling beside the gate to notify hotel guards of our return. We couldn't yank the rope any which-way, however. There was a pre-determined rhythm to the rope-shaking and bell-ringing, a signal that would tell those inside if it was friend or foe.

Those who were going out and who were staying in the hotel knew how many times the bell should ring to tell if outside was safe or dangerous.

After a while, the first and the second repatriation boats departed.

Those who were ill were the priority, followed by pregnant women, small children, and eventually unmarried individuals. Single individuals feared being forced to stay behind to work as laborers. Rumors had been circulating that singles, especially boys, would be made to stay and work. Some boys hastily got married to any Japanese girls willing to save them.

Exhaustion and impatience became apparent on people's faces. This took its toll on the health of the elderly and small children who started to struggle physically. Japanese in camps throughout China fell ill one after another.

The autumn wind chilled me to my bones.

My father was frustrated.

A riot had occurred, and no one knew what would happen next under such circumstances.

He wanted his children on board a boat going back to Japan as soon as possible. He had five children, one of them an infant. He constantly tried to make arrangements, but their turn for repatriation would have to wait.

He took his elder son's hand in one hand and the second son's hand in the other and brought them to visit the waiting area for boarding. It was a miserable place overflowing with people suffering from any number of illnesses and diseases. In such horrible conditions, in a tiny room packed with people, it was natural that an epidemic would quickly spread.

He gave up and returned to our hotel-turned-camp. Then, unfortunately, both of his beloved sons came down with measles. The two brothers were lying in bed side by side. The younger son's condition was slightly better than his brother's.

My father ran to several camps and brought back the Mantetsu Hospital doctor, a Chinese doctor, and a Taiwanese doctor, one after another, to examine and help his sons.

Little by little the brothers recovered.

When they were fully recovered, all we had to do was await our turn to board. Just when my mother finally started to breathe easier her relief was quickly and cruelly extinguished.

On the morning of November 23rd, my younger brother died at the tender age of three.

As my mother had an infant to attend to, my father was watching and taking the boys to the toilet at night. One night close to dawn, after the brothers had woken up and had been taken to the toilet as usual, my father was sitting beside them, watching them drift back to sleep.

However, on that night, the younger one could not fall asleep.

"*Tottan*—daddy—sleep. *Tottan*, sleep with me."

"Daddy is fine. Don't worry. Go back to sleep."

My father urged him to sleep and lightly pat the quilt under which he lay. The young boy, however, insisted his father sleep with him. He even came out of the bedding and pulled his father's hand.

"Sleep with me." With this gesture, at once so serious and so cute, my father felt relieved that the boy had recovered and it would be alright to sleep with him. He lied down beside his son.

Since the start of the repatriation until that day, he had been too busy to get enough sleep. That night my father fell deeply asleep for the first time in a very long time.

An almost imperceptible light rain had started to fall.

By the time morning came, the rain was falling steadily.

The Crematory in the Suburbs of Tianjin

Water Sheep (son) Fire Sheep (father)
Born in 1943   Born in 1906

It was still raining the following morning. The gently falling rain only magnified the tremendous grief my father and mother were feeling.

Soon, the time came for the coffin to leave.

My father, with his son's coffin on his shoulder, walked out of the camp. The rain had by then slowed to a mist. This water from the heavens was purifying his son.

"The heavens," my father thought, "are purifying my own path in life as well."

Movies and stories about war always show the scenes of the scattered corpses of countless soldiers. However, the reality of countless dead bodies of innocent children and their mothers is crueler.

Like my family, those who had already arrived in the cargo train station in Tianjin in November of the year the war ended were lucky. Those who were able to then catch a boat back to Japan were extremely lucky.

Suffering was greatest in Manchuria and North Korea where tragic deaths were common. Many Japanese were forced to abandon their children or grandparents who were unable to make the difficult journey back to Japan. Those family members may have been left in mountains, at riversides, or at roadsides.

To find their way home these refugees were forced to travel under the light of the moon, in secret. An infant might put the lives of all group members at risk. Mothers desperate to silence their babies covered their nose and mouth until they died by suffocation, inadvertently or otherwise. Others just left their babies to their fate on the ground.

Abandoned infants were eaten by wild dogs, or if they somehow survived that, they would slowly succumb to starvation.

Even if the babies managed to stay with their mothers and arrived at the relative safety of a camp, there was not a single drop of milk for them. The only chance left for the mothers to save their babies' lives was to place them in the hands of the Chinese, a decision which would later haunt many of the mothers.

By now, 2016, most of the mothers who lost their children have passed away.

The cry of their babies must have echoed in their ears throughout

The Crematory in the Suburbs of Tianjin

their lives and set them on a quixotic quest to find their lost babies. These journeys only ended when the mothers finally passed away themselves, a final ending to a deep gnawing grief and pain that they had carried their entire lives.

The babies left with Chinese families, after more than half a century, have grown up to be middle-aged individuals in China, many still searching for their lost mothers.

If Japanese civilians had had the chance to repatriate before that bitter winter, so many innocent lives would not have been lost, and many other babies would not have been abandoned.

Still, even under apparently far better circumstances, so many—especially infants and middle-aged women in their 50s and 60s—were dying in our camp.

It was such an extraordinary time. When a family member died, the best most could do was clip some hair and nails and bury the body in a shallow grave. In fact, it was a common sight. Camp members would drag the body to vacant land and bury it there.

It was the best they could do to console the souls of the dead. So everyone had thought my father would do likewise.

However, my father could not give up his idea just because everyone else was leaving the bodies of their deceased loved ones in these ways.

Our repatriation community tried to stop him from doing anything foolhardy, reminding him of the riot and other dangers, but my father would not listen. He knew the dangers from the start. There was no doubt about the great danger.

What would happen to a corpse buried under soil in the cold weather of November? It would be dug out and whatever the body was wrapped in would be stripped off. Clothing did not last long on a lifeless body.

Then, it was only a matter of time before wild dogs set upon it.

My father had a reckless character. Once he made a decision he resolutely stuck to it. He could not compromise his convictions. It was his weak point as well as his strength.

So at his moment of greatest despair, he made his way with iron determination. This crisis probably revealed his inner nature more than any other time.

Against all odds, he ventured into dangerous post-war towns where people said Japanese would never come back alive. He went out alone, on foot, with his son's coffin on his shoulder. The memory of that day is still etched on my mind.

How far was it to the crematory in the suburbs?

There was no military anymore to protect the Japanese. Besides, it was not a town he was familiar with. He was not even sure of the direction.

He could manage to stop a *yangche* rickshaw and ride on it, but it only went from one back road to another. But the driver would not go the full distance. For once, my father's powers of persuasion failed him as the driver feared for his life.

"Please, I beg you. I will pay you as much as you wish," he said, placing his palms together in a gesture of supplication.

But the driver would only reply, "My own life is more important than money." Carrying a Japanese would put the driver in grave danger.

Begging or haranguing even would not change the driver's mind.

There was no time.

His only choice was to get off the vehicle that provided some measure of safety and walk alone. As he came to the edge of the town, soldiers on guard duty suddenly emerged pointing a gun at him. Some fired warning shots from the distance, probably assuming he had a bomb in the box.

He was stopped and questioned by sentries and policemen several times.

Each time he put the coffin on the ground, explained the situation, gave them some money, a large amount of it, and bowed to them. One sentry looked at my father with pity.

"Are you a Japanese beggar? You are alone for a funeral, and on foot. Japanese people used to travel by car and pass here bursting with pride. I cannot take money from a beggar," he said, and let my father pass.

However, such great fortune was short-lived. At other places, he had to pay his way through a series of questions and warnings. Merely being questioned, however, was relatively peaceful.

A little later a bullet knocked his hat off and whistled past his head. It was a narrow escape, but not enough to make him turn back.

"I must do this," he thought.

He continued as if under a spell.

The Crematory in the Suburbs of Tianjin

He finally managed to reach the crematory in the afternoon. To his surprise, the first person he encountered there was a Japanese woman. The woman, however, looked more surprised than he was.

Given the conditions of her region, she had not expected any visitors. As the rain still drizzled under a somber sky, a tall, thin man was standing with a coffin on his shoulder.

She hastily went back into the house.

A short man in his 50s came out to see what the gaunt visitor wanted. Understandably enough, he initially refused my father's request.

From the end of the war, cremations had stopped. They had thought, under such circumstances, the crematory's inactivity would continue indefinitely. The furnace with its six gates contained some rust, so it would take some time to get it working properly. To run it, much firewood would have to be prepared.

After an animated exchange, the man told my father to wait and went into a back room to speak with someone. When he returned he said it would take at least six hours if my father still insisted.

My father was at a loss. Going back in the dark would be even more dangerous.

He offered to pay as much as they wish, and they finally agreed to finish the cremation in three hours.

My father urged him again and again to complete the work as quickly as possible. They said they could and asked him to wait outside.

He strolled around the old building, waiting.

The rain had finally stopped.

A weak ray of sunlight squeezed through the fading clouds and reached the earth. As my father walked to the back of the building, he found abandoned ashes here and there. Pieces of bones were scattered among the blackened ashes. Artificial teeth were glittering black. There were no gold or silver teeth, of course.

All kinds of thoughts passed through his mind.

He had come to the continent as a young man with an adventurous spirit, never imagining he would eventually return to Japan with such sorrow.

If he had achieved a dream of becoming king of the continent, traveling throughout the land leading a group of mounted bandits, he would have accepted the consequences and not even minded dying alone.

However, he could not stand the regret of having involved, and lost, a child. The undeniable fact of his son's death made him feel anger rather than sadness. The anger might have actually been a kind of self-loathing for ever marrying and becoming a father.

"Bao Taibao! Should I have entrusted my boy to you?" He recalled how Bao Taibao had frequently asked my father to give him his younger son. My father shouted his anguish toward the heavens that exposed more and more blue sky.

He could not even let go of his son in death—so how could he have entrusted his boy to the head of the bandits while he was alive?

Bao Taibao was also the head of the enemy that had attacked and completely destroyed Maidazhao Station where my father was stationmaster. Nevertheless, my father remembered Bao Taibao with heart-aching affection. He wanted to see him. He needed him more than anyone else. He thought, more than anyone else, he could share his sorrow with Bao Taibao.

Ha! Ha! Ha!

He could feel his hearty laughter booming from the clouds.

'Stationmaster,' he might have said, 'I warned you. Having two boys is unfair. You should have let me have one of them. I would have raised him to be a great man. But never mind now. Regret is meaningless. Stationmaster, don't be weak. That is not who you are. Your son is a part of yourself. Or rather, he *is* yourself. On this land where you have spent your energy, you will leave your heart…"

That's what Bao Taibao would have said, or so my father felt.

He was kept waiting for a long while. A cool evening breeze was blowing. The afternoon seem to drag on forever. Very soon it would be dark.

Thinking it was about time, he went back inside the building. The coffin was still on the ugly stand in the center of the room. The silence was ominous, as if the building had stood uninhabited for over 100 years.

He felt irritation, wondering how long they would keep him waiting, but also felt relieved to find his son still lying there. He had often held his son in his arms and tried to comfort him. When the boy got fussy, he found comfort in his father's strong arms and fell asleep.

Like those times, my father put his son's body into the coffin very gently, as if he was trying not to wake him up. Then he stretched his arms outward, took a deep breath, and as if trying to end a nightmare shouted, "Somebody, *please*."

The small man who had met him some hours before appeared and announced, "Okay, we are now ready."

Finally, it was time to gather the bones.

From the back of the house that had appeared deserted, two more people—another man and the woman he had met previously—emerged to help my father carry the bones. They were surely moved by pity for this forlorn man and his deceased child.

The small box soon became full.

However hard my father tried to push the remaining bones into it, they would not fit. Reluctant to leave the rest of the bones there, he could not resist scooping some up with his hand and stuffing them into his pocket.

"Thank you very much. I am deeply grateful," my father said sincerely to the three.

He displayed raw gratitude, with great relief, to have his son's cremation completed.

"I am amazed that you made it here alone," the woman said thoughtfully. "It must have been heavy. It will be easier to go back."

"Heavy? No, I didn't think it was heavy at all. I did not even notice the weight. That may be because he is my son."

The short man was also kind to my father.

He said he would like to offer a small gift of a free cloth to wrap the white wooden box with a prayer to repose the boy's soul, along with a discount.

If my father was in a usual state of mind, he would have refused a gift, even just a piece of cloth, for his own son's funeral, considering such a present and discount would dishonor himself. He could have insisted, "No, I will pay in full. In fact, I will pay twice the price," but he accepted the offer.

His beloved son had become smoke and disappeared into the sky of a foreign land. At the moment that he had to bear the worst pain of his life, fate had brought him these three people.

My father was very grateful for their kindness.

Just as occurred on the way to the crematory, he was interrogated and encountered dangers several times on the way back.

The sentry who had been sorry for him, calling him a Japanese beggar, seemed to have told the new sentry on duty that a Japanese man would come and let him pass. The new sentry on duty talked to my father.

"Hello. So, have you finished the cremation?"

"Yes, thank you. This is it," he said to him, raising the box wrapped in a white cloth to eye-level. The sentry quietly nodded and let him pass.

However, only that place was easy. At other places, even when it was the same sentry he had met earlier, a gun was pointed at him or he was again forced to answer the same series of questions before paying a bribe.

As it was getting dark, he put his hand in his pocket. He felt the faint warmth of the bones. It was comforting, as if he was holding hands with his son who had so recently been laughing and playing.

When my father finally arrived back at the camp, it was already past midnight. A man who had been waiting for him with great concern in the entrance hall unlocked the gate.

He immediately yelled at my father.

"Are you crazy? Walking around with a coffin on your shoulder! Everyone is talking about you. No one has dared pulling a stunt like that here. What a ridiculous thing you have done!"

Being yelled at upon arrival, after completing such a difficult journey, my father had no patience. He shouted back, "Did you say *ridiculous*?"

When the man saw the box wrapped in white cloth that my father held, he softened and said quietly, "All went well after all. But didn't you care about your own life? You still have four other children."

Indeed, it was a reckless act. If anything had gone wrong, for the sake of one lost soul, another life could have been lost while burdening the remaining family members with the task of carrying on without him.

The Crematory in the Suburbs of Tianjin

Under such circumstances, it was truly a blessing that he returned alive. The heavens must have recognized my father's sincerity and protected his life, not only for his sake, but also for us, his wife and children.

When he showed up after the cremation, an atmosphere of surprise and relief immediately spread throughout the hotel. Although it was midnight, people gathered in our room.

Some bowed prayerfully before the white-wrapped box, quietly wiping away tears.

However, I was very curious about the box.

At every meal by mother placed an offering beside it while saying a brief prayer.

My parents had learned a lesson from the death of their son. To protect their youngest they took the child to doctors at various camps. They would leave no stone unturned to protect the life of the baby.

Like various other incidents that happened in those days, I could have forgotten about the white-wrapped box soon after that, but on the contrary, it became an image that did not disappear from my mind easily.

To a surprising extent, this memory has most vividly imprinted on my mind. Small girl though I was, I took on the role of carrying the white-wrapped box containing my brother's ashes.

As our boarding day finally approached, we moved from railway hotel doubling as a camp to another camp close to the harbor. It was a military storage area. Here we would wait for our departure day.

My father carried bags with food and minimal clothing for the family on his back, front, right, and left. On top of that, he was holding hands with his elder son who had finally recovered. Since the death of the younger son, my father became even more careful. He never left his only son alone.

My mother carried her baby on her back, holding bags of baby's clothing and diapers in both hands.

My sister was much smarter than other second graders. She had a small knapsack on her back. She might have never imagined until that day that a knapsack could be used for something other than commuting to school.

I, a crybaby, was just clinging to the diaper bag my mother was holding. After all, it was only me whom my mother could ask to carry the box of bones.

"Okay? You are a good girl. Please pay extra attention and carry this home," my mother said, tying the ends of the white cloth firmly around my neck.

My mother might have felt sorry asking a kindergartener to hold and protect her baby brother's ashes. It was also her strategy to place a mark on me in case I got lost.

To me, it was a very serious issue. It was the first responsibility I was given in my life, and it marked recognition as someone who could be entrusted with a task.

At first, I cradled the box so tightly that I could hardly move. With a grave expression on my face, when I moved my body even slightly, I fearfully held the box with both hands as if handling delicate glass artwork.

However, such extreme caution didn't last. As my tension gradually dissipated, annoyance for being burdened with something heavy around my neck replaced it.

Besides, I could not see down around my feet well, making walking difficult. Fearfully I moved it slightly to the right, and slightly to the left. Then before I knew it I became emboldened to loop it around a single shoulder while holding it under one arm as if it was the water bottle I carried on school trips.

Each time my mother saw me carrying it in that position, she silently placed the box back to its proper place, in front of my chest.

After a while, I noticed that people's behavior changed around me.

When people saw me, everyone stopped for a second and gazed at me. Some quietly placed their palms together to *gassho*, a sign of solemn respect. Others shed tears and said "Good girl," patting my head, or hugging me. Some came to me quietly and placed the box back to its proper position as my mother did.

Soldiers stood straight right in front of me and saluted me in a formal manner.

It made me feel good. I intentionally paraded around the camp with it. Each time I ran, the box made faint knocking sounds as it bounced off my chest.

However, as those sounds became more and more familiar to me I gradually lost interest in the wooden box covered in white cloth. I became less curious about it.

Perhaps I unconsciously sensed its great importance. I held it tightly, never taking my eyes off of it.

One day, out of the blue, over 60 years after the end of the war, my mother, who was now over 90, said while gazing into the distant past, that she wished she had hugged him a lot more often.

A few days before he died, when my mother had been preparing breakfast, she heard small footsteps. As she looked back, she found Masaji, her youngest son, standing there.

"Mommy."

"Oh, dear, what is it? Pee-pee?"

"Pee-pee with Daddy."

"Right. Pee-pee with Daddy. Because you are a boy."

My mother crouched down before Masaji and calmly hugged him.

"Mommy," Masaji said to her again.

My mother stroked his hair and said, "Now go to sleep a little longer. I will wake you up when breakfast is ready."

He nodded yes, and said, "Mommy," for the third time, and walked back to the room.

During repatriation, he was always on my mother's back. He had been protected by the warmth of his mother's back. Then after his sister was born, the role of taking him to the toilet changed to his father.

"Daddy, pee-pee. Daddy, pee-pee," he tried to wake his father up shaking him with his tiny hands. But his father, who had been running around all day, was in a deep sleep and could not be woken up easily.

Even though he was so young, he must have felt sorry to wake his father up. That was why, on the morning of his last day, he kept saying "Daddy, sleep. Daddy, sleep."

"I should have hugged him more at that time. He was lonely."

The image of her precious three-year-old son, frozen in time, stayed etched on my mother's mind until the day she died.

Tanggu

Finally, our boarding day was decided.

After that, days at the cargo station were even busier with paperwork for repatriation and final packaging of our baggage. However busy my parents were, they remained consumed by the grief over losing their son. As our departure day approached, their sorrow grew deeper.

We are leaving our precious child behind on land which we will never again visit...

Each time my mother saw a boy of the same age and height cheerfully running around the camp, she stopped walking and gazed at him, briefly paralyzed by the memory of her loss.

At such times, my father would walk to the child with long strides and suddenly hold him up or sit him on his shoulders and ask, "Boy, how old are you?" or "What's your name?"

Without waiting for an answer, he would put the boy down and say, "Okay, good boy. Go home safely. Be careful, okay?"

The boy would look up at my father with a blank expression. After patting the boy two or three times on the head, my father would watch as the boy walked away.

As our boarding day was decided, my father purchased food for us—rice, flour, sugar and oil. With those ingredients, my mother cooked a large amount of *karinto*, a Japanese deep-fried snack.

He put the rice into cloth bags and then put one into a large knapsack. He planned to carry it on his back while holding the other bags on both sides of his body.

He could only imagine the condition of a defeated country and what life would be like there. His own experience of the war was intense, on the front line and on the continent. But how would he and his family live after landing in Japan? Japan was their homeland, yes, but it had changed drastically.

There were various rumors in the camp. People were saying strong bombs which the world had never seen before had been dropped on Hiroshima and Nagasaki. They heard that those bombs were different from regular ones; they would flash intense light in the air before exploding.

People further said that no grass or tree would grow for 60 or more

Tanggu

years on the ground where those bombs exploded.

The rumors were many: The U.S. Army plundered and committed acts of violence whenever and wherever they desired; the Japanese people were living under a tyranny severer than life in the repatriation camp and were not even allowed to go out; young girls had to be given up to the American military, like the military service obligation for boys. And if they refused? They would have their ears and nose cut off and their body torn from limb to limb. The Americans and the British were considered demons after all. No one knew what they would do to us.

Even though such absurd rumors were heard everywhere, my family's affection for their homeland was stronger than ever.

Japan might be in a miserable condition, but it's still our country. It's the Empire of Japan. We can manage after we go back.

That's what they told themselves in the end.

Rather than worrying about a future they could not imagine, people wanted to escape from their current misery as soon as possible.

For his final purchase, my father bought a big black leather trunk. It was a brand new, shiny case which still had a leathery smell.

"I have found something really nice. It is a high quality British trunk," my father said stroking it happily.

As a repatriating traveler, each person was allowed to carry 1,000 yen per person and all the baggage he or she could carry.

However, jewels, watches, and rings were not allowed. Although no photographs were allowed, ones showing someone in a military uniform were especially frowned upon. Photographs of humans or scenery were also strictly prohibited. Cash or forbidden goods that were hidden could immediately be detected by the scan of the baggage inspection machine.

Penalties for non-compliance were strict. If one member of a group was caught violating a rule, the entire group was not allowed to go aboard.

There were various rumors about the baggage inspection we all had to go through. Everyone fervently wished to get on board.

Besides illicit goods, the inspectors also searched for war criminals. Those who resembled a criminal or had a similar name were carefully interrogated.

When our baggage inspection started, my father was not yet with us. He had asked my mother to take care of our inspection because he was obliged to help others preparing to depart.

Helping others in the group finish paperwork necessary for embarkation, and confirming of the total number of people who would board, kept him busy.

His priority was not his own family. He always seemed to be away at important times leaving my mother anxious and nervous. After waiting a long time in line, it was finally our turn to board.

First my mother placed the large bag full of *karinto* she had made the night before on the inspection desk, and then loaded a wicker trunk, the leather trunk, and knapsacks. As we were allowed to take only baggage that we could carry ourselves, she had as much stuff as she could handle.

The Chinese inspector was slightly surprised to see such volume. He looked inside a bag and found it full of brown-colored, pinky-sized *karinto*. He did not know what they were and frowned as if our crispy snack was something disgusting.

My mother's heart was beating fast.

However, the inspection was not strict like rumors had claimed. The inspector moved on.

Next the brand new large British trunk was opened. Inside were the winning clothes that my mother had chosen after careful consideration. My father's angora wool shirts and pants, my mother's squirrel leather shawl, and other items that looked expensive were picked up and put aside one after another.

It was not really an inspection, but rather opportunity for the inspectors to take whatever they wanted.

Last he found some colorful kimonos on the bottom of the trunk. These were the celebratory kimonos made when my sister was seven and I was three. My sister's was a stunning sky-blue, long sleeved kimono designed with traditional noble coaches, and my kimono was red designed with flower baskets and *temari*, embroidered girls' toy balls.

The inspector picked up our celebratory kimonos quietly and nonchalantly dropped them behind the desk. This prompted a silent response from my sister who bit her lower lip and clenched her fists. My response, however, was not so quiet.

I suddenly screamed as if set ablaze while running toward the inspector.

People around us were taken by surprise and, not knowing what had happened, their eyes zeroed in on the direction of the shriek.

The place fell totally silence.

"*Your* kimono! *Your* kimono!" I shouted. In a flash I went behind the inspection desk, grabbed my kimono, found my sister's and grabbed that one as well, and then came back crying, dragging our kimonos.

People watching the whole scene held their breath.

My pale mother felt her whole body go numb.

"It's over," my mother thought, "they will stop us from boarding."

While my mother and the other Japanese waiting to board must have been surprised, the person who surely felt the most shock must have been the inspector. It was normal for them to take anything they liked, especially the most expensive goods. That was part of their good fortune as inspectors at that particular place and time. In fact, the inspector was wearing several watches he had taken from passengers on his wrists.

Everyone had been opening their baggage fearfully, quietly eyeing the inspector take whatever he wanted, mainly clinging to the hope to be allowed passage back to Japan. Everyone tried to keep moving without giving the inspector a chance to say a word that might lead to denial of our passage home.

However, that facade was broken by one small girl who furiously charged the inspector. The fact that she had a white box hanging from her neck might have helped.

I had said "*your* kimono" when I meant "*my* kimono," as was my habit since infancy. However, in this case, it did not matter whether I said "my" or "your," or said it in Chinese or Japanese. No one would have noticed the difference. The meaning was crystal clear. The small girl had reclaimed her precious kimono.

The Chinese inspector froze and gazed at me for a moment. The silence seemed suffocating as no one dared even breathe. After an eternal pause, the inspector slowly turned his body and, as if nothing had happened, turned to the Japanese soldier who was working as his assistant, and signaled to bring the next family.

U.S. Military Landing Craft (LST)

On December 25th, 1945, we went aboard the U.S. Military Landing Craft (LST) at Tanggu, an outer harbor of Tianjin. The staircase to its deck was long. People who climbed the stairs with heavy baggage on their backs desperately tried to not lose their balance, sometimes crawling on hands and knees.

It probably took several decades before people could look back and begin to make sense of their days on the Asian continent. In those turbulent final days, Japanese who were hurrying to get back to their homeland had no chance to feel a proper farewell. All they felt was the profound relief of finally being on board and getting back to Japan alive.

If they had managed to make sense of the years spent there they would have surely come to feel gratitude for the unwavering Earth. Acts of war like the Liutiaogou Incident and the Marco Polo Bridge Incident, and the subsequent years that passed may have seemed monumental but, in another sense, they were nothing but mere sparks. They might have caused some boulders to teeter and fall off a high mountain, but in the end they could not shake the planet that nurtured humanity, Earth.

Having remained stable and firmly grounded, the Earth endured the storm and waited for the day when beautiful green buds would reemerge. The vast, endless earth has always been the source of all power. It was a force beyond human affairs; it did not sway.

On the ship heading back to Japan, passengers were laying here and there curled up between their baggage. That was all the space they could finally obtain after a long, long journey of escape.

Even though they might have been forced to lay on the hard iron plates used to carry war tanks now stored in the hull, as a place leading them to their homeland, it brought them peace of mind.

I craved a deep sleep that would heal my exhaustion. My father surely felt the same. With his extraordinary physical strength and toughness, he had been working more than the rest of us. Only the unconsciousness of sleep provided a respite from his busy life. He should have had the chance to completely relax and catch up on sleep. However, he could not rest even after boarding the boat. He was assigned to distribute meals, take care of sick passengers, and was even asked to patrol on deck.

A temporary toilet was setup at the edge of the deck. However, it was only surrounded by a low wall without a roof and was hence completely

U.S. Military Landing Craft (LST)

visible from the bridge of the boat. The passengers, especially the women, were very reluctant to use it in the daytime, and waited until night fell.

But at night you could see the black winter sea rollicking ominously below your feet, making you feel lost in an alien world. Such fear was not unfounded. On the night the boat left China, a woman lost her footing and fell into the deep dark sea. She fell overboard around midnight. The boat was sailing at full speed. There was no way to help her.

Her shrill scream lingered.

Going to the toilet was risky.

Then there were rumors. Some said that when a woman went to the toilet at night, a human figure would appear. Others saw a female figure going up to the upper deck.

Even if those rumors were true, attempting to find out who it was or capturing the person could cause even more trouble. So it was decided that four strong men, including my father, would take turns watching on deck.

My sister, now a second grader, rushed onto the deck as soon as she got on board, played golf with other children and with American soldiers, or loudly recited multiplication tables toward the sea breeze.

"I can't wait to go to school!" That was what my sister, a model student, always said.

My father took his elder son wherever he went, as if the boy was his own shadow, never leaving him alone. He had become even more doting than he was at the camp. In the early days of the voyage, whenever my father's turn for watch duty came, he would say, "Now boy, let's go" and put his 5-year-old son on his back and stand up.

Others who thought father and son were playing together were not pleased.

"What? Do you think you are horses? You two are always together. How about leaving your son at least when you are on duty?"

"We're what? Horses? Are you calling us horses?"

"It's just an analogy."

"Even if it is just an analogy, we are not horses. This child is a treasure. My treasure. What if something happens to this ship?"

The critic did not back down. "It's bad luck to talk that way. What do you mean by *anything*?"

"Anything means anything. Anyway, this is my treasure. I cannot leave my treasure for a second."

My father was very serious, but a thin, tall man carrying his 5-year-old son on his back while patrolling the deck of a ship looked rather odd to the passengers.

On the second day of the voyage, a baby died. He had already had a fever before getting on board, but his mother kept that secret. As his fever rose, he refused milk. The end came shortly thereafter.

Around sunset, the small body was wrapped in straw matting, tied with a rope, and slowly lowered down into the sea from the stern.

The small bundle swayed right and left over the sea, as if the baby inside was shaking his head, and was gradually lowered through the surface of the sea.

The winter sea, which shone in a leaden hue, rolled and swirled and eventually swallowed the wrapped body which made its descent to the icy depths below.

The boat turned wide around it. The whistle to signify grief sounded long thereafter. The forlorn blaring brought many passengers to tears.

While those present at the funeral-like gathering were praying silently, the baby's young mother was standing in a stupor. As time passed, one passenger left, then another, and another. Finally, the mother was left standing there alone even as darkness fell over the ship and the sea.

As the voyage continued, many people started to suffer from seasickness. The waves of the Genkai Sea just north of Kyushu became violent.

The boat's hold was full of people. The stuffiness of the place made us feel as if we were being broiled. During our early days on the ship, I was having fun. I followed my sister to the deck, played with other children, or kept watching the waves without getting bored. We even ventured closer to the big American soldiers; it was our first time to encounter American soldiers. However, my seasickness worsened, and finally I laid flat like a dried-up frog beside my baby sister in the bowels of the boat.

Every time I dozed off, I somehow had the same dream.

Buried somewhere in my flittering consciousness was awareness of the ship swaying between and over the large ocean waves. In the

U.S. Military Landing Craft (LST)

distance, beyond the big waves, I could glimpse the pale face of the *hina* doll, swaying with the waves while smiling elegantly. I thought she must have been hot in the fire, but then, she must be cold in water now. I felt I had to save her by getting her up onto the ship. I would try to reach out to her, but she was always beyond reach, silently disappearing into the waves. After a while, she would once again reappear in the distance, always moving side to side, caught in the motion of the waves.

I hastily tried to reach her, but again she silently disappeared.

On the grayish blackish waves, the vivid golden dress of the *hina* doll appeared and disappeared again and again.

My mother also started to suffer from sea sickness. Worse, she could not produce breast milk anymore.

The dry biscuits with confetti that we received on board got stuck in her throat. No food was distributed for babies.

The image of the baby buried at sea remained in my mother's mind. "My own daughter will suffer the same fate if this situation continues" she gloomily thought.

When her first daughter was born, she did not know what to do with so much milk. Now getting even a spoonful of milk was more difficult than scooping water from the Milky Way. "What a contrast," she thought.

She recalled the early days of her marriage in Harbin and time spent with many Russians. One family had had a farm with a cow in their neighborhood. The next door neighbor was the widow of a Russian aristocrat. She wore black from the top of her head to her toes. It was rumored that she would wear mourning garb for the rest of her life.

This old Russian woman was where the abundance of milk came from. We received some every morning. The milk was too much for her to drink, so she bathed her baby in milk. Using milk for a bath now seemed like a shameful waste of precious food.

My mother felt determined to persevere. She grabbed some rice from the hemp sack, put it in a metallic wash bowl, and took it to the American soldiers who worked as cooks in the kitchen.

With gestures she tried her best to explain her wish to have it cooked. An American soldier kindly agreed and pointed to the watch on his powerful, hairy wrist. He then motioned at the time for her to come back and pick it up.

Her idea was to chew the white rice until it had the consistency of gruel, and then feed the baby with it. She was desperate.

From the start of the voyage, my mother and other Japanese women on board changed their view toward the American crew.

The Americans and the British had been feared for their cruelty and hated among the Japanese as if they were demons. In reality, however, the young soldiers were gentle and kind to them. When the women encountered them on a narrow passage on the ship, the soldiers always stepped aside, and they let the ladies go first through the doors.

The Japanese women, including my mother, had been living in a world where men were always above them. Moreover, they had lived through a war during which people said, "Give way to the soldiers." So the attitude of "ladies first" amazed and delighted them.

At the promised time, my mother went back to receive the cooked rice from the American soldier, who handed it to her with a smile.

She thanked them again and again, received it, and lifted the cover.

Expecting the warm tasty smell of freshly cooked white rice, she took a deep breath. It was not, however, the aroma she had been longing for. "Huh?" she mumbled in surprise.

The rice in the bowl was black, or brown… or rather chocolate color.

To the mother who had come to him with a desperate expression, the American soldiers had decided to give her a real treat, the best foods that they could imagine.

In those days, Japanese could never get their hands on ingredients such as milk, butter, chocolate, and cheese, no matter how desperately they tried. Chances were as good as plucking stars out of the Milky Way. The soldier had generously added such precious ingredients, and cooked the richest rice dish ever out of his sincere goodwill to please her.

However, my mother wanted to just eat a handful of plain white rice. She had thought a small bit of rice would help her regain her health and produce a drop of breast milk for the baby. Instead, we had chocolate rice. My father said, "Oh, this is tasty. Hey, son, it's good. Eat it, go ahead." He ate it and really liked it.

"America is great. They eat such tasty meals. No wonder they won the war. America will lead the world from now. Hey, let's go to America."

U.S. Military Landing Craft (LST)

A moment later he noticed my mother's expression. "Oh, what's your mother so upset about?"

It was only natural for her to be upset. On her long and hard repatriation trip, her train had been bombed and derailed repeatedly. After they managed to arrive in Tianjin, she spent days with great hardships at the camp, struggling with the anxiety of not knowing if or when they could go home. Finally, they managed to get aboard a ship back to Japan. Her only hope at that time was for her and her family to arrive safely in her home country. Now her husband started talking about another overseas adventure, this time one to America.

Looking at the faces of his father and mother in turn, my brother did not know what to do. His father was encouraging him to eat the chocolate rice. He wanted to, but his mother did not look happy.

At that time, looking at the chocolate rice, my brother was wondering what America was like. He could not have imagined that he himself would go to America a mere decade or so later after graduating from university.

In 1945, on the last day of the year that the war end, the U.S. Military Landing Craft arrived at Hario Seaport of Sasebo.

Arrival at Hario Seaport in Sasebo

Hario Seaport in Sasebo

At 10pm on the evening of December 31st, 1945, our ship entered Hario Seaport of Sasebo, Nagasaki Prefecture. Upon arrival, health officials doused us from head to toe with DDT, the herbicide used at that time as a disinfectant.

After inspection at the port, we traveled seven kilometers to the camp which was the former naval barracks, men on foot, women and children in a truck. Overseeing this movement became the last transportation duty for my father. Since joining Mantetsu in 1933, my father had devoted his life to transportation, dealing with cargo, military, and passengers.

Even though Nagasaki is in southern Japan, the night wind on New Year's Day was frigid.

By the time he sent the last truck off, the color of the sky had begun to brighten.

I did not get on the truck. Instead, I was carried to the former Naval hospital in Omura. My symptoms were too serious for seasickness, so appendicitis was suspected. To avoid the tragedy of a burst appendix, urgent hospitalization was arranged for me. There in hospital I was left all alone for the first time in my life. I had never been separated from my family. Even during our repatriation journey, I had not felt anxiety or fear, even for a moment. Because I had always been with my sister and brothers, protected under the expansive wings of my parents, I knew no state other than security.

Suddenly, however, I felt as if I was left all alone in the desert.

Far from a desert, however, the hospital was full of injured or sick soldiers in white hospital clothes, some laying still in bed gazing at the ceiling, others leaning against the corridor wall muttering to themselves while others absentmindedly moved their bandage-covered legs out from under blankets.

An urgent medical check showed that I did not have appendicitis, but my seasickness was so severe that my body had become very weak. I was to remain hospitalized until I regained physical strength.

Although there were many soldiers who were ill or injured, I was given a bed at the back of a room. I went totally rigid in my bed out of an unbearable fear.

A crybaby too preoccupied with her own fear to remember to cry!

Arrival at Hario Seaport in Sasebo

The soldiers were all kind. I was very anxious, but a young soldier with crutches took the trouble to come by my bed to tell me kindly that my sickness would be gone after taking some rest. "Take it easy and sleep," he told me.

During my week in hospital, my mother attended to me.

Many years later, I wondered how she could have come from the camp in Sasebo to the naval hospital in Omura where I was staying. There was no public transportation like busses. She might have been able to catch a short ride from the busy camp, but that seemed unlikely. So how did she get there?

I didn't realize until several decades later that my mother walked all the way to the hospital without stopping—with a baby on her back.

My father, walking around Sasebo with the English trunk he had bought in Tianjin, finally found a shop that carried horse gear. At first he was mistaken for a shopper who had come for food, or for a salesman, and was treated abruptly.

"Please wait. I have come here as I hear that the best craftsman in Japan is working here," my father said.

"The best craftsman in Japan?"

"Yes. Is the best craftsman in Japan here today?"

On hearing the phrase "the best craftsman in Japan," the shopkeeper opened his small eyes that looked like he was sleeping behind his glasses, and said, "That's me."

Then, hearing my father's request to make a *landoseru*, a leather backpack for schoolbooks, his thin eyes opened wide in surprise.

"A *landoseru*? Did you say a *landoseru*?"

In the town that had turned into a burnt field in the aftermath of the war, there was no shop selling *landoseru*. If you had no sibling to give you a hand-me-down *landoseru*, boys had to make do with cloth shoulder bags while girls used handmade cloth handbags. There was no leather, especially for a brand new, *landoseru* anywhere.

My father visited each shop where he might have such a bag made for me.

The best craftsman in Japan was initially surprised to have an order for a *landoseru*, but after hearing details his surprise turned into motivation. In the end, rather than merely saying that he would be willing to make one, he asked my father to let him take on the task.

"Considering your height, the bag for your son should be extra-large," he said, looking up at my father.

"No, it's for my daughter. Please make it regular size," he answered.

My father had found one fabulous *landoseru* for my sister for when she entered the local elementary school. He had kept the memory of the red *landoseru* displayed in the center of the bag shop window run by a Japanese man in Hohhot.

My father said to the best leather craftsman, "It's for my daughter, so I wish it was red or dark red."

"No, black is best. Black is the best color for anything. Formal kimono is black, isn't it?" the best craftsman in Japan said.

He thoughtfully looked at the English-made trunk and stroked it, and then said, "This is a Western product, and it's brand new. Where did you get this?"

Hearing that my father bought it in Tianjin, the shopkeeper said, "So, you have returned from the continent. You must have endured great hardship." As the two men warmed to each other, the shopkeeper said, "It's a pity to destroy such a high-quality trunk, but, alright, I will make a great *landoseru* out of it."

He agreed to take the job.

Relieved to hear that, my father then headed for Nagasaki. He wanted to see the town with his own eyes. After the atomic bomb attack, Nagasaki had fallen into ruin. Around the destroyed Urakami Cathedral were scattered fragments of the Virgin Mary statue with her face charred black, stone statues without heads, and torsos without limbs.

Military Policeman Miyamoto and his wife Naoko, who were from Nagasaki, remained fresh in his mind. He stood in front of the cathedral and looked down on the town of Urakami thinking of Miyamoto, Naoko, and their child.

I was happy they had gone back to Japan and wished them a quiet life in this town, never expecting an atomic bomb attack. Miyamoto, I am so sorry for you. I had wanted you to see your child, the beautiful boy you had always wanted. *The father and son who never met in this life. And Naoko – are the three of you living happily together in the next world?*

Despite the destruction all around him, he was reluctant to leave.

My father came into the room with a shiny black *landoseru*. He sat on the side of my bed and produced a small *mikan*—a Japanese tangerine—on a twig with a leaf. After seeing large-sized fruits like Nankou persimmons and Xuanhua grapes, the *mikan* with a leaf looked very small to me.

My father peeled it, and put a piece into my mouth. I found the sweet-sour taste very tasty. It was my first taste of Japan, and it might have been the taste of my father as well. Yes, the color of my father was bright orange, and his taste was sweet. That's how I saw him—a sweet and sour *mikan*.

My mother, in contrast, offered sustenance. My affection for her was my longing for her breasts. Her color was milky. Dozing in my mother's arms filled me with a sweet, warm and milky sensation.

When the last piece of the *mikan* was eaten, my father said happily, "This is your *landoseru*. You will be a first grader soon. Study hard like your sister."

My sister was always a model student at whichever school she attended, and was always praised by her teachers.

In Tianjin, on our repatriation journey, each time we moved to a new camp, my father immediately found a new school for my sister and took her there. She had always simultaneously attended multiple schools, two days at one school and three days at another.

As my sister walked to her new school with her teacher, my father called out in a loud voice, "Akiko, raise your head and put your shoulders back."

The teacher turned back and bowed with a smile, as if saying it was alright. She put her hand gently on my sister's shoulder and walked into the classroom.

At each school my sister was accepted warmly. She made new friends quickly. Of course it was mainly due to her bright personality. But there had always been more to it than that. Classmates accepted her warmly primarily because she was from the same country. She too was Japanese.

In a foreign land, this sense of nationality had strongly connected peoples.

My sister went to school in many unfamiliar towns. She sometimes got lost, but still studied cheerfully. My mother, who was worried about her, would wait for her come home at the gate of the camp while snuggling the baby.

Most students who had returned from foreign lands were required to repeat a school year. But my sister caught up with her classmates in her studies soon and smoothly passed with flying colors.

I decided to study hard like my sister. I wanted to cherish the *landoseru* for a long time to come, and I wanted to use it even after I entered higher grades.

Although I attended my entrance ceremony while staying at a temporary home without playmates or anyone I even knew, I was extremely happy. As soon as I saw the school gate, I slipped my hand from the sleeve of my mother's kimono and ran toward it.

That joy stayed in my heart. I loved my school and my studies. I attended all classes for the nine years of compulsory education.

However, my shiny new *landoseru* did not even last one year.

On my way home from school, I found myself surrounded by five or six boys. I've never figured out whether I had been followed or whether they had been waiting for me. The day was very cold, I remember that, so I guess it happened around the end of the second term of first grade, some days before winter holiday.

They might have been my schoolmates, but the boys who stood in my way were seniors I did not know. Two of them suddenly held my bag on my back from behind, and from right and left. The biggest boy took out a short sword called *higonokami* and with his full force he slashed the back of my *landoseru* in half. I had no idea such a fate would befall my treasured leather backpack.

Not imagining such an attack, I had happily worn it on my back while walking around my hospital room. Soldiers in white robes congratulated me and encouraged me to study hard. One day a thin hand from the bed in the center of our room beckoned me to his bed. I was a little scared and hesitated. The soldier with crutches in the bed across the room then signaled me with his eyes to go over to him. As I hesitantly approached,

Arrival at Hario Seaport in Sasebo

he gazed at me through hollow eyes, extended his bony hand and stroked my *landoseru* gently, showing his love. He nodded in silence and closed his eyes. A shiny teardrop ran down from the corner of his eye.

The next morning, he was no longer on the bed. Another injured soldier had taken his place.

About one week after the gaunt soldier passed away, a relative came to pick up our family. My mother told our nurse that I would be leaving the next day. The relative told me I was lucky to be in a hospital because it served three meals a day, something those on the outside couldn't rely on.

This comment made my mother understand the food situation in Japan.

In late afternoon, my father visited me with my sister and brother to prepare for leaving the hospital and to express his gratitude to our doctors and nurses. My little brother had not seen his mother for a while. After entering the door to my hospital room he quickly spotted my mother, cried, and dashed into her arms. "Hey, a boy shouldn't cry," my father said, smiling. My sister also wanted to hold her mother, but being older, she held back her emotion.

I wished all hateful crimes and evil deeds would disappear when day broke. Like the ominous dreams I had at night, I sometimes doubted that people could really be so cruel to each other. If the miserable war and the dropping of the atomic bombs, demonic deeds, had only happened in my dreams, they would have disappeared when dawn came. Then that hideously burning evening sun would sink to the bottom of the sea, wash and purify itself overnight, shudder its body, and reappear a refreshed figure the next morning.

From the next day, my father had many matters to deal with. Principally, he had to see to the survival of our family. He told me to be ready to leave hospital when he came to pick me up the next day. He took his son's hand in his right hand and his daughter's in his left, and walked down onto the road in front of the hospital.

My mother with the baby on her back, and I with my *landoseru* on my back, stood at the entrance of the hospital to see them go. My sister and brother looked back in turns to wave to us.

Even after we could no longer see them, my mother stood still and did not move to go back inside the hospital. Lightly patting the baby on her back over the blanket with her right hand, she held up her palm toward the setting sun, extended her fingers, and muttered something to herself. I could not hear what she was saying. Then I kicked a stone I spotted on the vacant lot beside the hospital.

After kicking it two or three times, a fun idea came to mind. I drew several squares on the ground, and, hopped on one foot while kicking the stone from one square to the next. I was totally absorbed in my game.

As I recall, those were my first footsteps on the island of Japan, my home country. I had been carried to this former naval hospital directly from LST. After that, I spent days in hospital, and I was finally discharged.

I was born on the continent. My memorable first step—or actually a skip—on my own country's soil was there. Of course, at that moment, I was so young, and so deeply engrossed in kicking stones, that I was oblivious to my momentous first step on home soil. And I paid no attention to my mother's explanation. What she said became clear to me only much later, after I had grown up.

My mother held her five fingers out against the evening sky and said:

"The thumb is your sister, the index finger is you, a crybaby, the middle finger is your first brother, the ring finger is your second brother, who was to be a great success, and the pinky is the baby. My five children are as precious as my own five fingers. Why was only this finger broken?"

She extended and bent her ring finger, showing her palm to the sky for a long time as the sun dropped out of view.

Taking advantage of the fact that she did not tell me to go back inside the hospital, I kept happily kicking stones.

Epilogue

After the war, my father lived as a martial arts master throughout his life.

With a firm belief that what was needed in his home country in the aftermath of the War was fostering the health and welfare of the younger generation, he opened a karate and martial arts dojo.

His dojo was Kenkokan Karate Dojo on Natsumezaka Street, the birthplace of novelist Natsume Soseki, northwest of the capital.

The first person my father would have loved to inform about the dojo was none other than Sanbo Toku, a demon on the Kodokan judo mat and a god to my father. However, he had already passed away. On March 10, 1945, while helping people trying to escape from raging flames caused by the Great Tokyo Air Raid, he died in the fire with them.

As the master of Kenkokan Dojo, my father advocated *"Dokuji gyo seiki,"* Spiritual Development of Individuality in Mind and Body. He saw this as the way to put judo into action in everyday life.

A practitioner should train himself by making a sustained effort of basic practice in order to realize the nature of the self. To make use of the teachings, he should find a suitable practice, and then cultivate and develop his spirit. That spirit is summarized by the phrase, *"Dokuji gyo seiki."*

The dojo, located close to Waseda University, attracted many aspirants of fine character. University students and many other practitioners who became impressively skilled gathered at the dojo to train, then over time left it as birds leave their nest. At the head of this pack of impressive students was my father's most beloved aspirant, Tokuichiro Tamazawa, who later became Director General of Japan's Defense Agency and the Minister for Agriculture, Forestry and Fisheries.

Many others from Waseda University also joined the dojo including Keizo Obuchi who later became Prime Minister, and Katsumi Yorimoto who later became the Dean of the Department of Politics and Economics and an authority on garbage disposal. Mr. Yorimoto had a great interest in environmental problems from his university days. At his farewell party held in the dojo before his departure to a university abroad, he made a great speech on environmental issues.

My father was truly blessed to be surrounded by sincere and diligent aspirants. I wish I could someday tell him that each of the aspirants who

Epilogue

started their practice in his dojo has become productive and successful.

My father's first son, Masayuki Hisataka, moved to the U.S.A. after graduating from university. It was the mid-1960s, when a dollar was 360 yen and when Japanese could not go overseas freely for personal travel. A group of family and friends saw him off with three cheers before he flew out of Haneda Airport alone.

Truly following in his father's footsteps, he performed a karate demonstration representing Japan at the 1964 World's Fair in New York. He performed *"kusanku,"* the same form our father had performed at the martial arts competition held during the Manchukuo Foundation Festival.

Our father was very pleased that both he and his son had the opportunity to perform at international judo demonstrations. He boasted of his beloved son who had grown up to be an amazing man at every opportunity.

Next, Masayuki performed a demonstration at the 1967 World Expo in Montreal, and remained in the city after the event. There he taught Kenkokan Karate and Kodokan Judo.

He also taught at various educational institutions including Colombia University, the State University of New York, McGill University, Loyola College, National Theatre School of Canada, St. Jerome's University, and the United States Military Academy in West Point—all while teaching at his own dojo. He devoted himself to teaching Japanese martial arts, barely sparing time for sleeping and eating.

Since then he has been passionately teaching Kenkokan Karate and Japanese martial arts worldwide in Europe, Russia, Australia, and Africa. He has received the following accolades:

Honorary citizen of Baltimore, U.S.A.
Honorary Chieftain of Asawa, a Native American tribe in Canada
Baron of Russia
Honorary citizen of Tbilisi, Republic of Georgia

In his final years, my father enjoyed spending time with his beloved first grandson, Hiroshi Hisataka, the first son of his eldest daughter.

The grandson was the son of my father's beautiful Harbin-born daughter he was so proud of. At home, my father treated him gently like any other grandfather and grandson, but at the dojo my father treated him severely, as a martial arts master would treat his disciple.

The first grandson became the last beloved aspirant to learn from my father. Later, on seeing Hiroshi's karate performance, my father's old students said he resembled their grandmaster, making them feel nostalgic for their younger days.

On August 13th, 1985, my father's life ended at the age of 82.

His funeral was held two days later on August 15th, which was, curiously, the last war-end anniversary day of the Showa era.

The memorial service for the war dead was attended by Emperor Showa for the last time. My father's funeral was conducted at exactly the same time.

Before attending the National Memorial Service for War Dead as a Diet member, Tokuichiro Tamazawa paid a visit to my father's funeral and saw him for the last time. I wonder how happy that must have made my father.

Chief Cabinet Secretary Keizo Obuchi also laid beautiful flowers and incense at his grave.

Many of his students attended his funeral. Some of them received the news of his death while traveling and changed their summer holiday schedule to attend. His beloved aspirant, dentist Yutaka Hayakawa, expressed his condolences with sweat trickling down his forehead.

On January 7th of the year 1989, Emperor Showa passed away.

Chief Cabinet Secretary Keizo Obuchi announced the name of the new era: "Heisei."

"Father, if you had been here for a little longer, you could have lived in four eras, Meiji, Taisho, Showa, and Heisei," I said to him. And then I heard his voice: "No, you don't understand. I couldn't go after His Majesty the Emperor."

He was right. He was always the trailblazer in the Showa era. On the continent, he paved the way and arranged the railroads for the military and devoted himself to military transport.

He departed at the end of the Showa era so he could arrange the railroad to the stars for His Majesty the Emperor.

Epilogue

The following line was written in a message of condolence.

"One of the few genuine martial artists in modern Japan has just left us."

Even after my father died, Tokuichiro Tamazawa continued to warmly watch over Kenkokan Karate dojo and supported the competitions and other events.

Prime Minister Keizo Obuchi also telephoned us.

As I happened to answer the phone, he said to me, "When Minister Tamazawa is out traveling abroad and you need to talk about the dojo, please call me." The prime minister's kind words moved me and I hastily expressed my gratitude.

My father's Kenkokan dojo is supported by many of his followers and the second generation master Masayuki Hisataka.

They are currently successful masters of Kenkokan Karate Do in their respective countries, namely:

Shunji Watanabe, U.S.A.
Masaki Enomoto, New Zealand
Wayne Donavan, Canada
Scott Brown, Australia
Michel Laurin, U.S.A.
Luce R. Campbell, Canada
Olaf Lotze, Germany
Sandra Leoni, Germany

"Mantestu-kai" (Mantetsu Society) was formed after the War for the purpose of supporting and seeing to the welfare of the former employees of the South Manchuria Railway Co., Ltd. and their loved ones. It also served as a network for members to exchange camaraderie and friendship.

In 1982, with donations collected by former Mantetsu employees and the family of the deceased, "The Memorial for the Souls of Mantesu Workers" was erected in Fuji Cemetery located at the foot of Mt. Fuji. The stone monument reads:

Memorial for the Souls of Mantetsu Workers

*For those who undertook their mission in Mantetsu
and devoted themselves to leading the great work of
Asian development, that they may be commemorated forever.
This is to enshrine their souls to maintain the spirit of Mantestu
and transmit it thousands of years into the future.*

April 1982
Mantetsu-kai, incorporated foundation

Since the erection, a memorial ceremony has been held annually in spring. As my father is also enshrined on the tablet, I attended the memorial service to offer my prayers. I have also assisted at the reception counter for the event.

Azaleas were in full bloom in the park as a refreshing wind blew through the lush environment.

Then I witnessed the last day of the Kako (Kahoku Traffic) Mutual Aid Society.

Like Mantetsu Society, Kako Mutual Aid Society was formed to support and see to the welfare of former workers after the War. The office for the Society was in the same building as Mantetsu Society. I often visited them to learn about those days.

As time passed, there was no way to deal with the aging of the members and the drastic decrease in numbers. After half a century of operation, Kako Mutual Society was dissolved on March 31st, 2001.

Prior to that, a dissolution assembly was held at Hotel New Akao in Atami. I attended the meeting with my father in mind. I wanted to witness the end of Kahoku Traffic.

The dissolution assembly proceeded in a somber atmosphere. With "The Glimmer of Firefly" being sung by all attendees, the Kako Mutual Aid Society completed its history.

Beyond the faraway Great Wall, two shining parallel black rails of Kahoku Traffic silently lay in a straight line before disappearing under the clear blue sky of the Mongolian dessert.

Epilogue

A memorial service for the late Lieutenant General Hiroshi Nemoto, former Commander of the Mongolia Garrison Army, was held on June 6th, 2003.

It was organized by Mr. Haruo Atsumi, President of Rakuda Association, attended by the family and relatives of Mr. Nemoto, the veterans' association of the former Mongolia Garrison Army headquarters, representatives of the former Mengjiang United Autonomous Government, and others who were successful in Mongolia in those days. I took part in the event as one of the 40,000 Japanese who escaped from Zhangjiakou at the end of the war.

My mother had always said to me, "We could withdraw in safety thanks to a great commander-in-chief." So I wanted to attend the memorial service.

I was received by the family of Mr. Nemoto at Koriyama Station. All the attendees went to his residence in Sukagawa City to visit the alter on which the urn with his ashes lay.

Hung beside the alter was a picture taken when he was leader of the 27th infantry of the Asahikawa 7th Division. He was being spoken to by the Emperor at a large-scale special military drill. The Emperor's white horse looked a vibrant and shining white that made me wonder if the picture had really been taken so many years ago.

They served us lunch, and then we went to the family grave of the Nemotos.

The memorial service in front of the grave proceeded smoothly.

In 1949, Lieutenant General Nemoto escaped to Taiwan. Japan was still under occupation by the United States.

Lieutenant General Nemoto, who had risked his life in repatriation of the Mongolia Garrison Army and the 40,000 Japanese at the end of the War, was again risking his life by escaping to Taiwan to support Chiang Kai-shek. Chairman Chiang Kai-shek had stated, "Never repay hostility with violence," and had made his best efforts to support the repatriation of the Japanese.

To repay his great deed, Lieutenant General Nemoto joined Chairman Chiang Kai-shek's Nationalist Government Army to fight in the Battle in Kinmen, fighting against China's Communist Party, and helped lead

Chiang Kai-shek's Nationalist Army to victory.

My mother maintained my father's dojo for 20 years after his death, and quietly passed away of natural causes at the age of 95 on July 2nd, 2008.

After attending her funeral, I made a trip alone to Nagasaki. There I visited the former Naval hospital in Omura where I had placed my first footstep on the land of Japan after my repatriation journey arrival at Hario Seaport in Sasebo.

Seeing the spot of my first landing in Japan after so many years, and standing there again, all seemed like a dream to me.

The Hario Port was renovated as "Uragashira Repatriation Memorial Peace Park." After passing through inspection at the port, people walked on the seven-kilometer road from there all the way to the former marine barracks. The grey building and its heavy atmosphere has been rebuilt as colorful Huis Ten Bosch, a popular tourist attraction that is lively and crowded with people.

In the Peace Park, a repatriation museum has been built, where items from that era are exhibited.

On the monument square, the statue of peace, a goddess, is standing tall facing the sea, still waiting for the souls of many Japanese to return. It reads:

The statue of peace
stands on the cliff at Hario Seaport,
shining on the ship that never returns

1941

1942

1944

1949

1941

1955

1962

Afterword

On this occasion of the 70th anniversary of the World War II, I have written this book remembering my father in his youthful days on the continent.

Unfortunately, we were not allowed to take home any referential materials or pictures when we repatriated. It was very difficult to learn how people lived at that time.

However, I have always had an interest in the era of the Sino-Japanese War. I researched myself, and have met many people to learn about that era. Thanks to them, I have gradually learned how life was, piece by piece.

I would like to express my appreciation to Mr. Haruo Atsumi, President of the Rakuda Association, Mr. Kesanosuke Ishii of the Industry Division of the Mengjiang Government, Mr. Naotoshi Ishida of the Ministry of Interior of the Mengjiang Government, Mr. Gisaburo Watanabe of headquarters of the Mongolia Garrison Army, and Mr. Kazuo Kuriwada of the Information Division of the Mongolia Garrison Army, among others.

Mr. Junpei Yasutomi, Director of the Kako Mutual Aid Society, received me each time with photocopies of publications and newspaper articles, as well as maps of that era, and kindly told me about the Kahoku Traffic and Mongolia of that time.

I would like to extend my gratitude to many others. Mr. Mikio Hayashi, President of Bunseisha Co., Ltd., has helped me publish this book. I deeply appreciate his support.

Finally, I would like to express my heartfelt appreciation to my daughter Yoko Abe and my nephew Hiroshi Hisataka.

August 13, 2015, the anniversary of my father's death

Sachiko Hisataka

About the Author

Sachiko Hisataka

Bio
Born in Zhangjiakou, China in 1939.
Repatriated to Japan with her family at the end of World War II in 1945.
Graduated from Shinjuku High School in Tokyo, and Gakushuin University.
Was employed by Gakushuin University.

Books by the author
Martial Arts Master KORI HISATAKA: My father's life in Manchuria
Originally written in Japanese, this book describes the younger days of the author's father Kori Hisataka at the time of the Second Sino-Japanese War and throughout World War II.

Sorazo Wasurenu
Sorazo Wasurenu won the *Oku no hosomichi* (Basho's *The Narrow Road to the Far North*) Literature Excellence Award. This memoir of the author's trip to Kyoto she undertook out of her longing for the purified world of poems created by female poets in the late 19th century also contains Japanese classical poems.

www.ingramcontent.com/pod-product-compliance
Lightning Source LLC
Chambersburg PA
CBHW062215080426
42734CB00010B/1892